DOGS

DOGS

Derek Hall

CHARTWELL
BOOKS, INC.

Published in 2009 by
CHARTWELL BOOKS, INC.
A division of BOOK SALES, INC.
114 Northfield Avenue
Edison, New Jersey 08837
USA

**Copyright © 2009 Regency
House Publishing Limited**
Niall House
24–26 Boulton Road
Stevenage, Hertfordshire
SG1 4QX, UK

For all editorial enquiries, please contact
Regency House Publishing at
www.regencyhousepublishing.com

ISBN-13: 978-0-7858-2523-4

ISBN-10: 0-7858-2523-1

Printed in China

Originally published as
The Ultimate Guide to Dog Breeds.

The Publisher wishes to thank the owners of the
various dogs featured in this book.

CONTENTS

INTRODUCTION 8

INTRODUCTION

Mankind's relationship with the dog can be traced back thousands of years, and it is indeed probably our oldest non-human companion. Excavations of Middle Eastern fossils, believed to be at least 12,000 years old, reveal a touching reminder of the bond between human beings and dogs, for on this site was found the skeleton of a dog lying next to the remains of its master.

Interestingly, for an animal that has been so important to us for so very long, there is uncertainty as to the exact way domestication of the dog occurred. We cannot even be absolutely sure of the evolutionary route by which the dog itself came about – although most experts are in agreement that the wolf is its most probable ancestor. Later, we shall look in more detail at the most likely theories concerning dog evolution, and some of the ways in which the dog may have begun to befriend human beings will be explored.

DOGS OF MANY KINDS

Despite the huge variations in size and appearance, all breeds of domestic dog belong to a single species, *Canis familiaris*. No other species of animal in the world exists in so many different forms, and this is because the majority of breeds have come about as the result of man's almost ceaseless attempts to create the perfect dog for every task and every fancy. The smallest dog breed in the world today is the Chihuahua. It measures no more than 9in (23cm) in height and weighs a maximum of 6lbs (less than 3kg). At the other end of the scale is the Irish Wolfhound, a gentle giant that towers above the Chihuahua and can reach 32in (81cm) or more at the shoulder, and which when standing on its back legs is taller than an average-sized person.

Between these two extremes can be found a bewildering array of diverse breeds. Some are built for speed or endurance, and others are designed to guard people and property – just as they have done for centuries. Some are prized for their herding abilities, and others for their skill in detecting or retrieving game for the hunter. But despite all of these admirable working qualities, many dogs are owned simply because they fulfil another important

LEFT: Dogs make wonderful pets for people of all ages, not least the elderly. They offer protection, encourage activity by asking to be taken for walks, and even help people cope with their disabilities.

OPPOSITE: The Labrador is one of the first choices when it comes to training dogs for the blind. It is noted for its equable temperament and faithful attention to duty.

role for man – they have adapted perfectly to become good and faithful friends. In this, the dog excels like no other animal. Intelligent, affectionate, playful, resourceful and loyal, many a dog would give its own life in defence of its owner, and for most owners, no expense or effort is too great to ensure the health, safety and comfort of their pet.

Today, there are about 400 different breeds of dog in the world. It is impossible to be exact about this figure, because new ones continue to emerge from time to time. Some dog breeds are common and familiar to many people, wherever they live. For example, many of us would probably recognize well-known breeds such as German Shepherd Dogs (otherwise known as Alsatians), Dachshunds (the familiar 'sausage dogs') or Greyhounds. But few people outside their native countries would be able to name with certainty such dogs as the Norwegian Buhund or the Neapolitan Mastiff – although many of these breeds are now becoming established in countries far beyond their original homeland as breeders seek to encourage wider ownership of more unusual breeds.

A breed is described as a purebred dog of predictable size and shape. What this means in reality is that if

DOGS

The Bernese Mountain Dog is a working dog, used for herding and pulling farm carts in its native Switzerland. It is an ancient breed, probably dating from Roman times.

two dogs of the same breed are mated, the offspring will look exactly like their parents, the offspring having inherited the genes that determine certain physical characteristics. They will also have inherited the parents' natural instincts. Therefore, for example, an Afghan Hound will have the tendency to hunt by sight, because the genes that determine this behaviour have been passed on to it by its parents.

Sometimes changes do manifest themselves during the reproductive process, some of which may be subtle, such as slight variations in coat patterns or changes in colouring. Other changes or mutations can be more profound; for example, a wire-coated dog may appear in a litter of normally smooth-coated dogs. Because characteristics are usually passed from one generation to the next, breeders have long sought ways of improving the line by selecting the very best examples from which to breed. So, for example, the strongest, fastest hounds will be mated together to maintain the qualities of the breed in the next generation.

Many of today's breeds have come about by crossing different types of dogs, in the hope that the offspring will reflect the best or most desired characteristics of each of the parents. Thus, for example, the Bracco Italiano came about as the result of crossing gun dogs with hounds to produce a breed with the best features of both types – in this instance, a pointing dog with extra stamina.

DOGS AND HUMAN BEINGS

Throughout recorded history, mankind's enduring association with the dog has been well documented in many ways – in sculpture, in art, on film and in literature. Art from the Babylonian Empire over 5,000 years ago, clearly depicts huge, mastiff-type dogs. There can be little doubt that these animals were valued comrades in battle and probably performed guard duties as well. Fleet-footed sighthounds, like Greyhounds and Pharaoh Hounds, feature as drawings on the walls of Egyptian tombs dating back to 4000 BC, indicating not only the presence of such breeds at that time, but also their significance in the lives of the people in those far-off times. Indeed, so important was the dog considered to be during this period that it was worshipped in the form of the god Anubis, who is represented as a dog-headed human being.

In the Middle Ages, dogs were frequently depicted in scenes, and the Bayeux Tapestry clearly shows Bloodhound-type dogs riding into battle with the Norman army. Later, in the 18th and 19th centuries, for example, it often seems that scarcely a painting was commissioned without a dog appearing in it somewhere – sitting patiently at its owner's feet, lying resplendent by the fire, or joining the hunters with their guns. Van Eyck, Gainsborough, Hogarth and Landseer are among the many famous artists whose work has helped to immortalize dogs in art.

More recently, dogs have featured in literature, and no one who has ever read Dodie Smith's *A Hundred and One Dalmatians*, or watched the film, will ever forget these endearing dogs and their antics, as they try to escape from being made into an overcoat by the villainous Cruella De Vil. Then there is Buck, the half-St Bernard, half-shepherd dog that is the hero of Jack London's bittersweet epic tale, *The Call of the Wild*.

Although many dogs make delightful pets, the huge range of breeds seen today has not come about because man wanted a bigger choice of

INTRODUCTION

Children love dogs and dogs love children. But children must be taught from an early age to respect all animals and treat them with kindness and sensitivity.

house companion! It is because most breeds of dog were designed to perform a particular duty, and the fact that many of them have friendly natures and adapt well to living in our houses as pets is something of a bonus. Although the need for dogs to carry out certain types of work has diminished, in other working situations they are still as valued and important as they ever were.

There remains to be discovered a better all-round detector of drugs or explosives than the canine nose, and police forces around the world would arguably rather have a well-trained German Shepherd Dog by their side than any other sort of deterrent when dealing with a rowdy gathering. Moreover, rounding up a flock of hillside sheep without the help of a dog, such as a Collie, would be an

DOGS

Dogs are rewarding creatures: they inspire love and return it with interest. In fact, 'loyal' and 'faithful' are the adjectives most often used to describe the dog's sterling qualities.

almost impossible task, while many who are blind would be facing an isolated and lonely future without the intelligent seeing eyes of a kindly Labrador. The list of such examples is endless.

Today, interest in dogs and all things canine is as great as it has ever been. As we find ourselves increasingly under pressure at work, or because of the tensions in the world, so the simpler things in life – like a relaxing country ramble with a dog – take on a greater significance. Dogs fulfil a need in a way that no other animal can; we need them and we feel grateful that they seem to need us, too. For people living alone, a

dog is a perfect companion, and for a growing family it is the instant playmate that expects to join in every bit of fun.

A well-trained and happy dog makes a loving friend: it is always willing to participate in whatever you want to do; it won't criticize; it won't sulk for too long if it can't get its own way; it guards the house and alerts you to visitors; it gets you out and about; and each has its own unique character that can amuse for hours. The therapeutic value of dogs is also well-known, and their usefulness in reducing stress and encouraging calm in people around them cannot be overemphasized. But it takes effort on

both parts, and a degree of dedication and a lot of common sense and patience from you, for this happy coexistence to occur. Choosing the right sort of dog is one of the most important aspects of ownership, and this is examined in more detail later on.

Inevitably, a huge industry has evolved to cater to our love of dogs, which, unfortunately, has not always worked to the advantage of dog or owner. Unscrupulous breeders have sometimes offered poor-quality animals, particularly if the breed is popular and in demand, which reduces the quality of the breed overall – especially if such animals are then bred on – and may even result in dogs with behavioural problems. Happily, it should be possible to avoid difficulties like this by buying only from a reputable breeder; on the positive side, there has never been more choice of potential canine pets or working companions available to the would-be buyer. Once purchased, every aspect of a dog's nutrition, entertainment and general well-being can be easily provided for, and companies even exist that

INTRODUCTION

specialize in offering holiday accommodation that will provide a welcome for our dogs, too!

The descriptions found later in this book cover over 170 of the most popular breeds from all over the world. They will hopefully provide insights into the varied world of dogs, helping you to choose the right animal for your own particular situation.

DOG EVOLUTION AND THE DOG FAMILY

The dog is a carnivorous or meat-eating mammal belonging to the family Canidae. The ancestor of all the world's meat-eating mammals (including the dog) is thought to be a small, primitive carnivore called *Miacis,* that appeared about 40 million years ago in what is now North America. About 30 million years ago, *Miacis* gave rise to a creature called *Cynodictis* which, about 10 million years ago, gave rise to *Cynodesmus* and *Tomoritus* – possibly the direct ancestors of the dog family. The development of the canid, or doglike group of carnivores, continued throughout the Pliocene and Pleistocene periods and in due course culminated in the appearance of the members of the present-day dog family.

DOGS

OPPOSITE: The wolf is the chief contender as wild ancestor of the domestic dog. Both have similar characteristics and form family/pack groups. So, in a gradual process, the socialization with man began, who realized that the wolf's hunting instincts could be conveniently harnessed. Thus began the probable evolution to wolf-dog, companion and working animal.

RIGHT: The Dingo is a feral or semi-domesticated dog with a sandy-coloured coat. It is a native of Australia and is believed to have been introduced by early aboriginal immigrants to the country. This example was photographed on the Nullarbor Plain of South-Western Australia.

BELOW RIGHT: The African wild dog is one of 37 species of the family Canidae, which also includes wolves, foxes, hyenas and jackals, among others.

By now, dog species had spread to all parts of the world – except for the southernmost regions, such as Australasia and Antarctica, from which they were isolated because of the vast oceans that separated the land masses at that time.

Today, the Canidae, or dog family, is represented by 37 different species, included among which are the foxes (of which there are about 20 species), the

grey wolf and the red wolf, the jackals, the raccoon dog and the African wild dog. (Dingoes, thought for so long to be naturally occurring wild dogs are, in fact, feral animals – in other words, domestic dogs that have returned to living in the wild.)

Somewhere among the members of the Canidae is the ancestor of the domestic dog, but which of them is it? The fox certainly resembles many of the modern dog breeds in general appearance, but it is not a pack animal and other factors – such as differences in chromosome numbers making the offspring resulting from dog/fox matings infertile – would tend to eliminate the fox from the list of possible ancestors.

Hyenas can also be discounted as potential ancestors, despite their superficially similar resemblance to dogs, since the evolutionary line that

The Golden Retriever has all the right instincts that enable it to search out and rescue survivors in difficult situations.

gave rise to them is different from the one that produced the dogs. Jackals and coyotes are very similar to domestic dogs, and crosses between dogs and these wild animals are fertile. However, there are sufficient internal differences between them to suggest that, although they are close relatives, they are not the same species.

This leaves us with the wolf. Although there is still no undeniable scientific or archaeological proof concerning the direct ancestor of the domestic dog, what evidence that does exist is strong enough for most scientists to believe that the dog lying by your fireside is in many ways no more than a highly evolved wolf. Let's look at some of this evidence: first, anatomical features of dogs and wolves, such as the teeth, show almost no differences; second, like coyotes and jackals, wolves and dogs can mate to produce fertile offspring. There are variations in the periods during which wolves and dogs come on heat, but these may have been caused by man's selective breeding of dogs. Perhaps more subjective evidence comes from our own eyes, and we need only take a look at a wolf before comparing it with a breed of dog, such as the Alaskan Malamute, to see the almost uncanny resemblance that exists between the two.

Other important similarities exist in the way in which both wolves and dogs behave. Each is a social pack animal, and even thousands of years of domestication has not been able to eradicate this behaviour from the domestic dog and, as we shall see later, it demonstrates this aspect of its nature in almost everything it does.

Even if we accept that the dog arose from its wolf ancestor, there is still some conjecture about the precise way in which this occurred. Is the dog simply a modified wolf that has come about through the production of countless generations of domesticated animals? If so, then not only have we seen domestication occur but also huge changes in the nature of the animal itself – far more than could be accounted for by natural evolutionary processes over this timescale. Thus, for example, we have seen the appearance of massive breeds, like the Wolfhound, and tiny breeds such as the Chihuahua. We have also seen the results of man altering the breeding cycle itself, so that the domestic dog now comes to maturity at six months or so, whereas the wolf is not ready to mate until it is at least two years of age.

Another theory suggests there was a wolf-dog mutant that directly gave rise to the domestic dog. It has even been proposed that the Asiatic wolf is the animal in question, and that it was first domesticated by prehistoric northern Asian tribes.

Domestication of the Dog

Even if all of the foregoing questions still await definitive answers, what is not in doubt is man's profound influence on the dog, who discovered in this animal the blueprint for a creature that would change his life forever. For the first time in our history, here was an animal that would become a friend and ally, rather than just another creature to be hunted or feared. Here was an animal that appeared intelligent, expressed emotions, and appealed to the human soul, and which became a vital piece of the jigsaw that helped man understand the natural world. While man was changing the dog, however, the dog was imperceptibly also changing the life of man; with the dog helping him, man could travel faster and more efficiently than before, and could protect his livestock and even his own life from marauding predators. In time, the dog became an invaluable helper in a multitude of different tasks. There is no doubt that the dog altered both the speed and the direction of human development, and helped set the pattern for a relationship that endures to the present day.

It is quite possible that domestication took place several times and in different locations throughout prehistory. Fossils of domestic dogs dating from between 8,000 and 12,000 years ago have been found in localities as widespread as Iraq, Israel, America, Turkey, Denmark, Switzerland and England, although it is thought that the relationship between man and dog may have begun even earlier than these finds suggest.

In the same way that there are uncertainties connected with the true ancestor of the dog, there is plenty of conjecture, too, about the way in which domestication actually occurred. Domestication, however it happens, is a slow process, and the affectionate, obedient, human-oriented dog did not suddenly appear on the scene; for this to have been achieved, generations of animals showing the propensity to socialize had to be selectively bred. Domestication is also different from tameness. Tameness can be taught to an individual animal, but this behaviour will not pass to the next generation. A domesticated animal, on the other hand, will produce offspring with the same traits as its parents. Once a domesticated dog puppy reaches a

certain age it will not only instinctively show friendliness towards human beings, but will actively seek out their company. Contrast this behaviour with that of, say, a natural-born hyena puppy of the same age, which will act aggressively towards humans and will do all it can to avoid contact with them.

The domestication of the dog is clearly more than simply a process whereby the animal and man became tolerant, even friendly, towards each other. As we saw earlier, man recognized in the dog an adaptable and versatile creature that was not only capable of becoming socialized but which also exhibited a variety of useful traits. These include the natural ability to hunt, to guard, to haul loads, and to retrieve. By carefully selecting animals with desired traits and breeding for these qualities, man was able to produce dogs which excelled at certain tasks. One could say that this was the beginning of the categorization of dogs into groups according to human needs.

But what is it about the nature of the dog that made it a suitable subject for domestication in the first place? To begin with, the dog was the right size to become man's companion – big enough to be a useful pack member, guardian, and hunting animal, while

being of a size that did not preclude it from living inside caves and other homes with human beings. The dog is also a strong, agile and alert animal with a powerful range of senses. It is able to breed fairly soon after it reaches maturity and produces a litter containing a useful number of offspring. Moreover, the dog is an intelligent creature with a willingness to do man's bidding, which not only meant that the task of training it could be achieved more rapidly, but also that the animal could to some degree bring its intelligence to the task in hand.

In all of this, we must remember that the relationship between man and dog is unlike any that exists between man and other animals, in that we recognize in the dog a willingness to please and a desire to cooperate with us. It is clear that the dog finds the process of living with man rewarding, accepting without question its place as part of the human 'pack', and receiving food, protection, shelter and stimulation in return. The dog also clearly enjoys the attention and love bestowed upon it by its human owner.

THE ORIGINS OF DOMESTICATION
Now let us look at the possible ways in which the domestication process occurred. Several theories exist that try

DOGS

to explain this, one of the most popular and easy to imagine scenario being when dogs began to scavenge around the edges of camps used by early man. Scraps of food discarded by man would have been taken and eaten by the dogs, in a 'clearing up' process that would have been beneficial to both. It would also have helped remove items that may have attracted rats and other unwanted food raiders. The dogs may have hung around close to the camp, and their barks would have proved useful in raising the alarm when any other animal or human intruder approached too near.

Over time, some of these dogs may have become less timid and may even

Among the many benefits of mankind's relationship with the dog was that man was enabled to travel faster than he would under his own steam. These Huskies seem to positively relish their work as they speed across the ice.

have begun to recognize humans as food providers; this would have been a

powerful factor in hastening the process of domestication. The dogs may even have accompanied man on his hunting expeditions, again hoping for a chance to feed off any leftovers, and it is even possible that some form of cooperation took place during the actual hunt.

It was possibly during this stage that human beings began to recognize individual dogs that showed more friendliness or more ability to be effective in the hunt or act as guard dogs, encouraging them by rewarding them with extra food and thus reinforcing the bonding process.

Alternatively, it could be that wolves or wild dogs were chased from their kills by stick-wielding or stone-throwing humans who, having taken from the carcase all they required, left the remains to be picked over by the animals they had chased away. In time, generations of these animals may have

DOGS

OPPOSITE: This German Shepherd (Alsatian) will eventually become a police dog, indispensable in many tasks that would be difficult or dangerous for its handler to accomplish unaided. Here the dog is being trained to deal with a potentially dangerous assailant.

RIGHT: Feral dogs photographed in Goa, India. These are usually animals which have escaped from a domesticated situation to fend for themselves, where they soon revert to the wild state. This can also occur in cats.

somehow come to regard humans as partakers in the hunting process.

It has also been suggested that the association started when dogs became companions for human beings. Orphan wolf cubs would have been raised by children as pets, for example – although the reasons why this would have taken place are somewhat hard to imagine, since the wolf was probably an animal to fear and would have been regarded as a competitor for food.

Whatever the actual process, the mutual bond between man and dog was slowly forged. Over time, dogs showing different traits came to be regarded as useful for different tasks. Thus swift, quiet dogs may have been chosen to accompany humans hunting timid prey, such as deer, while hunting wild boar,

and other strong or dangerous game, would have required the services of powerful dogs which could bring the prey down. Naturally protective dogs, whose alert senses caused them to bark at the approach of intruders, and which may also have been of impressive size, would have been prized as guard dogs, while the herding instincts displayed by other breeds would have been valued and developed, enabling livestock to be moved about more easily and guarded against marauders. It is hardly surprising, therefore, that the dog, with

so much natural talent at its disposal, should have been raised to the level of a deity by ancient civilizations such as that of ancient Egypt.

WHAT IS A DOG?
We have already seen that the dog is a member of the family of mammals Canidae, placed in a yet larger group of mammals known as the Carnivora or carnivores. Carnivores are meat-eating animals that catch their food by hunting, despatching and eating their prey using their powerful teeth and

INTRODUCTION

jaws. Other well-known carnivores include bears (which are closely related to dogs), cats, pandas, raccoons and seals. All the physical features of a typical carnivore are present in the domestic dog, although some have been selectively modified by man in certain breeds.

THE SENSES

As in many other animals, the brain of a dog is the command centre for its whole body. The brain controls and coordinates all of the body's functions, and the dog receives a constant influx of information from the sense organs in order to do this. Dogs are intelligent, social creatures with well-developed brains, capable of a wide range of different activities and with the ability to learn new patterns of behaviour.

It is the sense of smell, above all the dog's senses, that seems to us to be the most acute and remarkable, its ability to detect scent being up to 100 million times greater than ours, enabling the dog in the wild not only to track prey successfully, but also to read the scent messages left by others of the same species, informing it where territorial boundaries lie, of readiness to mate, and so on. Clearly, this amazing faculty was of importance in the natural selection of the dog, for such an animal would inevitably stand a better chance of survival.

The sense of smell is well-developed in most dogs, but in some breeds the ability has been blended with other attributes to produce, for example, superb hunters such as the Foxhound, the Basset, the Otterhound, and the Pointer. In order to maximize any scent it receives, a dog has a long nasal passage and special scroll-shaped bones in the nasal cavity, known as turbinates, which help increase the surface area of scent-detecting cells. It is likely, therefore, that dogs with a foreshortened nasal apparatus, such as Boxers, have inferior scenting abilities than dogs with longer muzzles. When a scent is passed to the cells responsible for detection, the message travels to the brain as an electrical impulse along the olfactory nerve, being received and processed at the part of the brain called the rhinencephalon. In addition, dogs have another structure in the roof of the mouth, called Jacobson's organ, which also detects scent particles.

As human beings, vision is regarded as our primary sense. In other words, we use sight to tell us about our surroundings before any of our other senses come into play. The role that vision plays in the life of the dog varies from breed to breed, but it is unlikely that this sense is ever as crucial or even as finely developed as in human beings.

In a dog's eyes, as in our own, the light-sensitive cells in the retina at the back of the eye are of two types: rods and cones. Rods are concerned with night vision, and a dog has many more of these rods than cones, which explains why it can see so well at night. The cones are responsible for high-intensity daylight vision, in which colour is important. The fact that a dog

has far fewer cones than a human being helps to explain why scientists have concluded that a dog has almost no capacity to see in colour.

There needs to be movement for a dog's vision to work effectively. You may have noticed that a dog appears to lose sight of someone standing still at some distance away from it. But it seems that the dog can again detect their presence once the person moves. The importance of being able to detect movement obviously has its roots in the natural behaviour of the wild carnivore.

Similarly, a stationary prey has a much better chance of avoiding detection than one that is moving in the dog's line of vision.

The manner in which the eyes are positioned in the skull varies from breed to breed and has a profound effect on the way a dog sees. Sighthounds, such as the Saluki, have narrow skulls with forward-facing eyes set close together and almost no stop. These features combine to give the Saluki, and others like it, excellent overlapping binocular vision – a vital aid when judging

INTRODUCTION

distance and focusing on the prey prior to going in for the kill. Many of the sighthounds, or gazehounds as they are also known, have a reputation for aloofness, which may partly be because they are more concerned with scanning the distant horizon for imaginary prey than concentrating on matters closer to hand!

By comparison, many of the sheepdog and retriever breeds have eyes positioned more laterally. In the case of sheepdogs, this would be an advantage when trying to keep an eye on wandering sheep or watching for predators that might attack the flock; for a gun dog, such as a Golden Retriever, widely-spaced eyes help it

The Borzoi is an example of a sighthound, or gazehound which, having a narrow skull and closely-set eyes, has excellent binocular vision, helping it to judge distance and pinpoint its prey before going in for the kill. Its habit of scanning the distant horizon gives it a reputation for aloofness which is not entirely justified.

to see falling prey more easily and thus make retrieval a quicker and easier task.

Interestingly, all puppies are born blind. Not only do their eyes remain tightly shut until they are ten or more days old, but the visual cortex in the brain is also so poorly developed at birth as to render them unable to discern anything from the light entering their eyes even if they were open. They rely on other sensations in these early stages of their lives, such as warmth and smell, to help them find their way about in the nest. It usually takes about six weeks before a puppy can see properly.

Good hearing is another of the features we associate with dogs, and it is certainly well-developed in canines. Again, hearing is a sense that dogs use to help them find their prey and avoid their enemies. Dogs hear sounds in the low-frequency range, but they are also able to detect sounds of much higher frequencies than can human beings. The ability to hear high-pitched sounds may be associated with prey detection, and it explains why dogs react to special dog whistles that appear silent to us. Just as a dog can distinguish between different smells, so also has it a remarkable ability to discriminate between different sounds that would appear almost the same to us. Thus a dog can tell the difference between the

footsteps of its owner approaching the house and that of a stranger doing the same thing, the first leading to signs of happy expectation, the second provoking a fit of aggressive barking.

So do dogs understand what we say to them? Clever though dogs undoubtedly are, it is unlikely that they have the capacity to actually understand our language. However, they are experts at both picking up the visual clues we adopt when we speak, and also at associating the tones we use when saying different things. For instance, we probably use a light, questioning tone when asking if a dog wants to go for a walk, and we may even make specific hand or body gestures as we speak. On the other hand, we would probably use a lower, sharper tone of voice if the dog is being scolded. We might also use dismissive arm movements, banishing the dog from the scene of its 'crime'. The dog, being a quick learner, soon comes to link your actions and voice with either a pleasant or an unpleasant moment in its life and reacts accordingly, giving the impression that it understands what we say. The ability of a dog to discriminate between sounds can go much further than this, of course, and many dogs are taught to respond appropriately to a variety of different

commands, such as SIT, COME, LIE DOWN, and so on.

Dogs have other senses, too, and like other mammals have receptors and nerve endings in their skin that can detect changes in temperature which can, for example, help them feel pressure or pain,.

DOG BEHAVIOUR

One of the great delights of dog ownership is to be had from observing your pet as it goes about its everyday life. By nature, dogs are highly social pack animals, having inherited and retained many of the behavioural traits associated with their wolf ancestors, and which are clearly seen in the domestic dog today. A dog will display these characteristics whether it is interacting with another of its kind or not, amusing itself by following a trail when out on a country walk, or in its behaviour towards its owner.

This last point is a particularly important one to remember when training a dog, for it considers its owner to be part of its pack, and in order for it to obey commands correctly, and deter it from trying to become the dominant member of the pack, the dog must first come to regard its owner as pack leader. As soon as a puppy is introduced into a household,

LEFT: When compared with the sighthounds, the Golden Retriever's eyes are placed more laterally, enabling it to spot falling prey more easily and making retrieval a simpler task.

OPPOSITE: This Border Collie is obeying the command to LIE DOWN or lie low. In the working dog, this is an important part of the herding instinct, in that it will assume a low profile to avoid alarming the sheep in its charge.

it starts to look for clues telling it where it stands in the pack hierarchy. During the time a puppy matures, it must learn that it ranks at the bottom of the pack, below all the members of its human family. This is important for everyone's future harmony, including the dog's, for a dog that considers itself to be in charge can become wilful and even aggressive as it strives to assume command. A young puppy must therefore learn, for example, that it cannot do as it pleases and that it must wait until everyone else has eaten before it gets its own food. Show the puppy, on the other hand, that you can do whatever you want to do, such as grooming it or sitting in its bed, and that the time for feeding is when you choose and not when the animal demands it.

It is important to reinforce the fact that you, and not it, are 'top dog'

during the time that the puppy is maturing. Make sure the dog ultimately obeys all your commands, even if it takes time for it to respond correctly. If you tell it to sit, keep pushing the hindquarters gently down while repeating the command until it complies. A rewarding word, and perhaps a treat, will help to reinforce good behaviour. Tug-of-war and rough-and-tumble games with your dog are fine, but it is important that they end

with you as winner. Remember, throughout your relationship with your dog, that firmness and kindness work better than anything else where training is concerned.

There are two types of behaviour that a dog will exhibit. The first is instinctive, and includes not only life-sustaining activities like feeding, but also the behaviour that make a dog a dog, such as mutual sniffing of rear ends when two individuals meet,

marking territory, a tendency to want to protect owner and property from intruders, the desire to sit next to you on the sofa, given the chance, and so on. Although an individual can be trained to modify or suppress some of these behavioural traits, they are deeply rooted in the canine psyche from birth.

The second type of behaviour is learned. Some behaviour is learned by all wild animals as they react with their environment, but a pet dog, subjected to so much stimulation and conditioning, will quickly acquire forms of behaviour designed to make its life easier – even if some of these are cunningly disguised as a desire to please others! For example, a dog is not born with the tendency to carry a newspaper to its master, but on learning that such an act results in praise, perhaps even in a treat, it may become a regular part of its repertoire.

Although there are many kinds of animals that socialize with others of their own species, the dog is one of only a small number that also socializes with different species, and it is perfectly happy to consider humans in a similar way. In fact, the dog's entire heredity is built around close cooperation as a means of ensuring survival, for example, hunting together to help bring down large prey and warning each other of dangers to the pack as a whole. The dog expects to be part of the group, which is why it is always ready to dash outside with the children or join in their games, and why some dogs left behind when you go out shopping become so miserable and even destructive. In its own mind, the dog is

unable to understand why it cannot go where the rest of the pack is going.

It would require a whole book to deal adequately with the complexities of dog behaviour, but here we have space to mention the subject only briefly. Listed below are some of the more common aspects of dog behaviour that are easy to observe.

PACK INSTINCT

The dog, as already mentioned, is a pack animal. Cooperative behaviour helps the wolf to capture large prey, and dogs retain this characteristic. This is one of the reasons why dogs make good companions; they fit into our lifestyles and happily go along with whatever we want to do, because they realize that this helps in their survival. The members of a wolf pack do not take kindly to wolves from other packs invading their territory, and neither do domestic dogs appreciate intruders – hence the frenzied barking and other signs of aggressive behaviour whenever a stranger approaches your home. Your dog is simply defending its pack and its territory.

The look of intense devotion on the face of a dog as it looks up at its master in the expectation of attention or food is another example of pack

OPPOSITE: This dog is gazing intently at its owners, willing them to part with food. However, it must be taught to mind its manners and refrain from making a nuisance of itself at mealtimes.

RIGHT: In order to facilitate its own survival, the dog will happily adjust itself to the lifestyle of its owner, even to the point of fraternizing with the family cat.

© Roger H. Goun Flickr creative commons

behaviour, and is precisely the way a puppy looks up at its mother.

COMMUNICATION AND BODY LANGUAGE

Communication is everything to a dog. Dogs acquaint each other concerning their mood, their willingness to mate or play, and their ownership of territory. They also show each other who is boss. Dogs use a variety of different methods to convey all of these and many other important pieces of canine information not only to other dogs but also to their owners.

Scent is one of the most powerful mechanisms of communication in dogs. Male dogs mark their territory by urinating, and may also 'wipe' soil or grass with the scent glands in their paws. A male dog will usually cock its leg and urinate on a part of an object some distance off the ground; this is intentionally designed to leave the scent at nose height for the benefit of other dogs investigating it. Dogs also urinate at intervals to provide themelves with an odour trail to remind them how to get home again, while droppings may be impregnated with an odour from the anal glands. The urine from a bitch on heat can tell other dogs in the area when she is ready to mate. Dogs, of course, read the scent from other animals, too, and use this when tracking.

The mutual sniffing inspection that takes place when two dogs meet – usually at each other's front end first and then at the rear – is another example of scent being used to convey information one to the other.

Your dog also uses its tail as a signalling flag, a furiously wagging tail being an indication of pleasure or excitement, while a tail held stiffly, with just the tip wagging, is more likely to be an aggressive posture and is often adopted when confronting an unknown dog. The tail can also be used to signal other moods, indicating submission when tucked firmly between the legs.

29

INTRODUCTION

raise a hind leg, and present its vulnerable belly. This posture is often adopted by your pet when acknowledging you as the leader of the pack – an action that also results in a pleasant tummy rub from you!

By contrast, a dog wanting to exert dominance will do all it can to make itself appear bigger. Ears, tail and hackles (the hairs running down the centre of the neck and back) are raised, the neck is arched, and the animal may even snarl. The dominant animal may try to reinforce its position by towering over the other dog or placing a paw firmly on its back.

PLAY AND ATTENTION

Play is an important part of a dog's life, especially when it is growing up. Many animals use play as a way of learning how to survive. Puppies play-fight with each other, and with their human family, as a means of improving their skills at defending territory and settling disputes. Toys often represent prey, and a puppy hones its hunting skills by dashing after balls and other toys, preventing them from being taken by running away with them. As they grow, most dogs seem to retain their playful instincts, and will often play just for the fun of it. Playing with your dog helps

The dog also utilizes a whole range of other body language. As part of the submission posture described above, a dog will attempt to make itself look smaller by flattening its ears, dropping its head and shoulders, and crouching. In extreme cases, to really make the point, it will roll over,

DOGS

OPPOSITE: Dogs love repetitive games which are also important for exercise, reinforcing natural behaviour and visual coordination. This Border Collie is waiting for its owner to throw a stick so that it can retrieve it.

RIGHT: It is fun teaching a puppy new skills, even if they are not particularly useful, like shaking paws! It does demonstrate, however, that the dog is one of the few animals which will happily socialize with us, sensing that its survival rests on its being a member of the family or human 'pack'.

to keep it stimulated and thus prevents boredom. During play, or in an attempt to get its owner or another dog to play, the play stance is often adopted. This involves the dog crouching down with its front legs bent but with its hind legs held straight.

This attention-seeking behaviour is one of many strategies a dog will use when it wants something. The fixed stare, accompanied by the furiously wagging tail, can tell us in no uncertain terms that supper or a walk are overdue, while a sharp, impatient bark reminds us that the dog has been outside for long enough and would now like to come in; a head pressed heavily on the knee or leg at mealtimes is a begging gesture (and not to be

encouraged!); a paw pulling or patting at our arm is also a way of attracting our attention; a toy dropped ostentatiously at our feet is another invitation to play. Obviously, you cannot always resist these pleas for attention, and so you comply. Do we train dogs or is it the other way round?

OTHER NATURAL INSTINCTS

We share our homes with our dogs and we treat them as members of the family. In some ways we even regard them as honorary human beings. But a dog is still a dog, despite domestication, and given a chance most dogs will soon show plenty of examples of basic

INTRODUCTION

canine behaviour. Breeds with strong hunting instincts, such as hounds, will dash off on the scent of possible prey – often oblivious to the 'return' commands of their owners. This instinct to hunt is so strong in Greyhounds that they are often muzzled when out walking, just in case they spot the local cat!

Digging is a form of behaviour shown by many breeds, especially terriers, and is often related to finding prey that has gone to earth. Some dogs dig to hide bones from rivals, or to dig them up again. Digging can also be an effective way for a dog to escape the confines of the garden if it has the urge to wander.

We have already seen how the strong guarding instincts of some breeds are put to use, and a dog that may appear submissive towards its family can become an aggressive and highly protective creature when

Dogs are social animals and after the first sniffing ritual is over like to play. One of them will usually assume the dominant role, and it is usually immediately apparent which one it is. By the look of its tail, the larger dog seems to be adopting the aggressive posture assumed when confronting another dog it does not know.

confronted by a real or supposed threat from a stranger.

The desire to mate can make dogs completely focused and uninhibited,

and male dogs (which are always sexually ready) can undergo a complete character change when a local bitch is on heat, much to the exasperation of their owners.

CHOOSING A DOG

Choosing to own a dog is a decision not to be taken lightly. It is an unfortunate fact that many have a hankering for dogs entirely unsuited to their own particular lifestyles or personalities, and a large, boisterous breed can be a disaster in a small urban flat. Although dogs are infinitely adaptable creatures, one kept in an unsuitable environment may not show its true character and may make life miserable for its owner, while there are many which should not own a dog at all. It is unkind to keep a dog simply as a burglar deterrent because you are out all day or simply because you like the look of a particular breed and regard it as some kind of status symbol. A dog is an intelligent, sensitive creature that needs to be properly understood, given the

A dog is very clever at getting what it wants, whether it be supper or a walk, when it will make its wishes known to us in no uncertain terms. Then, the only course of action is to don boots and overcoats and put on its leash.

INTRODUCTION

chance to express itself naturally, and become an integrated part of your life.

There are, in fact, several factors that need to be considered almost simultaneously when choosing a dog, but a start should be made somewhere! Some of what follows can apply to both cross-breeds and pedigree dogs, but the rest is more relevant to pedigrees, due to the fact that behaviour and characteristics of known breeds are easier to predict. Breed behaviour is possibly the most important factor to consider when choosing a dog. The breed sections that follow in this book are a useful way of gauging the

appearance and general temperament of specific types, as well as indicating the size of the dog (the height is measured at the withers). Some potential owners have no special breed in mind when deciding to own a dog, and the breed sections of this book may help them decide on a type they would otherwise never consider.

Unless you own and work a dog such as a sheepdog, the chances are that your purpose in getting a dog is because of the companionship it provides. The size of the dog is an important initial consideration, but some big dogs seem bigger than others!

Many dogs retain the urge to play, even in later life, enjoying having their bellies tickled, playing tug of war, or jumping into water to retrieve sticks. It is important to play with your dog in order to provide mental stimulation and prevent boredom.

A Deerhound is a big, tall dog that takes up a remarkably small space lying down, moving about the house with quietness and ease. Some large dogs, however, can seem like walking disaster areas in the home, liable to knock things off tables whenever they pass, while a St Bernard will make even a moderate-sized house feel small as it sprawls asleep across the floor. Interestingly, among the top most popular breeds in Britain and America are Golden Retrievers, Labrador Retrievers, Rottweilers and German Shepherd Dogs, none of which are exactly small!

Similarly, some big dogs have relatively modest appetites, whereas a few have enormous ones. The cost of feeding a dog is a significant factor, for even some medium-sized breeds can consume 330lbs (150kg) of meat a year, to which must be added the cost of mixer and other food items.

While on the subject of cost, remember that there will also be vet bills to meet for regular vaccinations

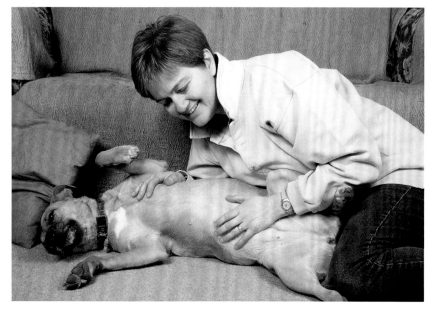

DOGS

dog the exercise it needs? Some toy breeds may be content with a ramble around the garden or a walk to the nearby shops, but many dogs – such as hounds and gundogs – will expect (and require) plenty of vigorous exercise, sometimes a couple of times a day, which will prevent boredom and keep them fit and healthy. Some breeds, such as Border Collies, need lots of interest and stimulation to keep them out of trouble, but provided they get sufficient exercise, most dogs will be quite happy to fit into your routine and will look forward to their home comforts.

Do you choose a male or a female? There is something to be said for either

and other forms of treatment, equipment such as collar, leash, name-tag, grooming tools, food and water bowls, treats, toys, bed, and possibly travelling cages and car harnesses. There may also be boarding kennel costs to meet when you go on holiday. It may be worth considering one of the many pet insurance schemes available, since the cost of unexpected veterinary treatment can be considerable.

Your lifestyle is another important factor: all dogs require some form of regular exercise, but some demand more than others. How much time and motivation have you got for giving your

INTRODUCTION

sex, and the choice will be purely personal. Males of a particular breed can be a little more aggressive and dominant than the females, and are usually more outgoing and bigger. Sometimes harder to train, males are also more inclined to be smitten with wanderlust – especially when a local female is in season. Females tend to be quieter, less aggressive and territorial, and are less likely to wander off. Unless neutered, females come into season twice yearly and may attract the attention of all the canine suitors in the neighbourhood. Many say that females make the more affectionate pets, but may be just a little biased!

Pedigree dogs are usually classified according to the tasks they perform – although many of these breeds today perform a role no more arduous than that of being the family pet, even if originally they were bred for hunting, guarding or other duties. In this book, the system of grouping dogs into six categories, based on their original uses, has been adopted, i.e. hounds, gun dogs, terriers, utility dogs, working dogs and toy dogs.

Some breeds make better choices than others, when it comes to temperament, especially where young children are concerned. Many small or toy breeds are not very tolerant of children, who may not realize how

DOGS

Be aware, when choosing a dog, that large breeds can present problems of their own in terms of the space they occupy and the amount they eat. Nevertheless, the German Shepherd is one of the most popular dogs around, even though it is not exactly small.

delicately a small dog needs to be handled, or be so boisterous as to frighten it. Terriers, on the other hand, usually relish plenty of rough and tumble, and seem to enjoy a busy, lively environment where children are around.

Exercise requirements notwithstanding, many members of the hound group can make good choices as pets, but a few, such as Borzois and Afghan Hounds, will not suit everyone, and giants of the group, such as Wolfhounds, tend to need plenty of space. Furthermore, some large dogs are also much shorter-lived than medium-sized or smaller breeds.

Many of the best-known pet dogs come from the gun dog group, in that they are easy to train and naturally willing to please, most adapting to life with a human family with ease and enjoyment. Among the ranks of this group we find such perennial favourites as the various setters, retrievers and spaniels, while breeds such as the Italian Spinone have in recent years also been gaining new fans.

If dogs in the utility group have a common link it is to have been used as guards. This characteristic is very apparent in some breeds, especially those that were originally bred for fighting. Although today this more pugilistic side of their behaviour has been bred out, the dogs in this group are very protective, although they can still make charming pets.

Dogs in the working dog group were usually bred for a variety of different tasks – either to herd flocks of domestic animals or to perform duties ranging from guarding to sled-pulling. From this group come some of the most popular pets, such as the German Shepherd and the Corgi, but there are also plenty of other, less well-known breeds that have yet to prove their long-term popularity as pets.

Generally, you can obtain dogs in one of several ways. First, if you are not concerned about getting a recognized breed, you can tour your local pet rescue centres. Here you will normally find a heart-rending selection of dogs – mostly cross-breeds (mongrels) – all looking at you with imploring eyes. Many of these dogs are already fully grown, so at least there is no worry as to how large the dog will eventually become.

This fact, however, reveals one of the other problems associated with 'rescue' dogs. The dog may have been mistreated or inadequately socialized, and many of its bad habits may not reveal themselves immediately and may subsequently be hard to break. Consequently, you may need to prepare yourself and your home for a few shocks during the so-called settling-in period! A dog with an unfortunate past may be nervous and insecure, at least to begin with, and this may manifest itself in behaviour such as bouts of howling or furniture chewing whenever it is left alone. Under no circumstances should you ever strike a dog if it behaves in this way. This will only make it more difficult for the dog to bond with you (a vital element in successful dog ownership) and may even cause it to attack you in defence.

Sadly, there are some dogs that will never be the confident and friendly animals they may have been in different circumstances. The other drawback with rescue dogs is that they may already be several years old, which means that your time together is going to be reduced from the start. Occasionally, dogs will be offered for homing simply because their owners have died, but it is more usually the

INTRODUCTION

case that they have either been abandoned or have been placed with the centre by owners not prepared to put in the effort required to turn a puppy into a well-adjusted adult dog.

Nevertheless, choosing and giving a second chance to a rescue dog can be a rewarding experience for you both, and with kindness and patience (and you may need to show even more patience than with a puppy) even the bad habits of an older dog can often be eradicated. Cross-bred dogs are invariably entertaining and intelligent animals, and their mixed parentage often expresses itself in a wide variety of different behaviour. Cross-breeds also enjoy what is known as hybrid vigour, making them less susceptible to the specific ailments that often affect pedigree dogs, and they generally seem to have robust constitutions.

When you see a dog that appeals to you at a rescue centre, you will probably be given the opportunity to walk it on a leash, but be prepared for your arm to be stretched! Rescue dogs, however well they may be looked after, simply cannot be given the same exercise and attention that you would give your own pet, and so they may be highly excited and desperate to get out. Don't let this exuberance put you off; most dogs will calm down once

they have made the adjustment to normal life. Use this 'getting to know you' period to see if you like the way the dog moves, if it shows sufficient interest in you and your family, and so on. It won't be a full test of its character, but it will give some idea as to your future compatibility.

Before you can take a dog from a rescue centre you may be required to fill in various forms, and some centres even insist on checking your home to make sure it is suitable for a dog. There will normally be a charge for obtaining a dog in this way. These are all good measures, designed to prevent dogs being homed with unsuitable owners. Most rescue centres neuter dogs before releasing them, and a vet will have examined the dog and inoculated it against canine diseases before it is even presented for adoption.

Although most of the dogs available from such centres are cross-breeds, the occasional pedigree sometimes turns up. Some centres may even operate a register, whereby potential owners can be put on a waiting list of people hoping to obtain an unwanted pedigree dog of a particular breed.

You can also obtain dogs from local pet stores and from

The striking-looking Dalmation, with its dramatic markings, should not be regarded as a mere fashion accessory. It is gentle but fun-loving, and excellent with children.

advertisements in magazines, local newspapers, and so on – especially if you are looking for a particular breed. Although many of the dogs offered for sale in this way are perfectly good and healthy animals, some are not, and it is therefore wise to do some research before making a purchase which may involve some considerable cost. Organizations such as breed clubs can provide lists of breeders in your area, and you can check to see if the advertisers are among those recommended by the club. In any event, if you looking to obtain an expensive pedigree dog, it is advisable first to discuss your requirements with several breeders if possible.

Try to have a list of questions written down before you call, so that you get all the information you require. The kind of things you might ask could include information concerning the breed's temperament; the cost of keeping the dog; how much exercise it will require; whether or not it is good with children; whether the parents have been shown and have won any

certificates; whether the puppy can be returned if defects are found; and when the next litter of available puppies is due. The answers to some of these questions may help you decide not only if this is the right breeder for you but also if it is a breed that will suit your needs. Let the breeder know if you are looking for a dog from which to breed, or if it is to show, or simply be a pet.

Having decided on a breeder, you should arrange to visit the litter, in fact more than once if possible. Always ask to see the mother; her temperament

The Jack Russell Terrier, although not universally recognized as an official breed, is small but brave and an excellent watchdog.

may provide clues about her offspring. Check to see that the animals are not showing signs of anxiety or any other

dubious traits. They should all look healthy and confident. Notice how the puppies react to you and their surroundings. Finally, you will need to make your choice, and you will probably know instinctively which is the one for you!

Puppies do not normally leave the litter until they are about eight or nine weeks old. During the time it is in the litter, the puppy will have learned basic pack behaviour and communication. But a puppy that has remained in the litter for more than 12 weeks may have begun to develop poor socialization habits. When you take your puppy, the breeder should provide you with full information about its vaccination programme, its diet, its worming treatments, and any other details that may help the puppy settle down more quickly in its new home. Ask about exercise routines, the best way to begin house-training, and advice on any other matters on which you are unsure. Most breeders are very knowledgeable and will willingly provide as much help as they can.

Whatever dog you finally choose, remember that it is going to be around for many years and will become an important part of your life. Treat a dog with kindness and understanding and it will repay you a hundred-fold.

WHAT TO LOOK FOR IN A HEALTHY PUPPY

Nose Should be cold and wet when awake, with no discharge or sneezing.

Mouth Breath should be pleasant-smelling, the teeth straight and white, and the gums pink.

Coat Should be clean and shiny, with no bald, itchy patches. Check for evidence of fleas.

Body Should be symmetrical and well-grown. Body movements should be agile and supple.

Ears Should be clean and pink inside, free of discharge or redness and with no unpleasant odour.

Eyes Should be clear and bright, and the under-lids should be a healthy pink. There should be no redness or watering.

Anus Should be free from swelling or irritation as well as being clean and dry.

Skin Should be clean and free from dandruff, blemishes, and sore patches.

Limbs There should be no evidence of lameness. The puppy should be able to stand squarely and be active and fluid in all its movements.

Chapter One
WORKING DOGS

This group of dogs includes more different breeds than any other, and being so large may be split into two smaller groups in some countries, i.e. working dogs and herding dogs. The first group features breeds that, between them, do a variety of work, for example, guarding, herding, carrying loads or pulling sleds and other vehicles, law enforcement duties, and rescue work. Some are bred to carry out more than one task. Thus, for example, the Alaskan Malamute may be a powerful sled-pulling dog, but its huge size and loud bark mean that it can also perform well as a guard dog. In addition to these roles, many of the dogs in the working group are among the most popular of pets.

The working dog group has within it animals of hugely differing shapes and dimensions. They range in size from the small Welsh Corgi, standing only 10–12in (25.5–30.5cm) high, to the giant of the group – the Anatolian Shepherd Dog at 32in (81cm). But although this huge dog is the tallest of

the group it is not the heaviest, and the Mastiff can weigh up to 190lbs (86kg). In spite of there being differences in vital statistics, what these dogs all have in common is generation upon generation of breeding that has brought them to the peak of perfection. Each dog, whatever its size, is ideally suited to the task expected of it, and many are indispensable servants of mankind. Most also share common traits of intelligence and obedience and have an inbuilt desire to perform the job for which they have been bred.

The history of herding dogs goes back thousands of years, when nomadic shepherd tribes adopted mountain dogs to act as guards, both to protect the herd from marauding wolves, bears and other predators, and to act as watchdogs to warn against thieves and other enemies. Thus the dogs had to be big, strong and courageous. Interestingly, light-coloured or even white dogs were favoured, since they could be more easily distinguished from attackers by the shepherds at night. The

majority of these mountain dogs carried mastiff blood, which no doubt gave them the fighting qualities so necessary for them to do their work. Among the best-known examples are the Estrela Mountain Dog, the Hungarian Kuvasz, and the Pyrenean Mountain Dog.

Later, as some of these mountain tribes began to settle in the fertile valleys and lowlands, the need for such large and often cumbersome dogs began to diminish. The requirement was now for smaller, faster and more mobile dogs that could keep large flocks of domestic animals together. Many of these dogs became the ancestors of modern-day sheepdogs, such as the various types of collies, as well as the quick-moving Australian Cattle Dog and the Lancashire Heeler. Some of the world's working sheepdogs are hardly ever seen outside their native lands, and the qualities that suit them for a life spent working with livestock do not always translate into suitability for the show ring or even family life.

The qualities required of a herding dog include the ability to control large flocks of cattle, sheep, goats or other livestock, and to quickly and obediently respond to the commands of the shepherd. It is also vital that the dogs are instinctively protective towards their owner and the animals in their charge. These traits, together with a high degree of intelligence and willingness to be trained, mean that dogs of this type also make excellent guard dogs. This is not to say that training is always a simple task, however. Many of these breeds are strong-minded and strong-bodied dogs that need some initial convincing that their owner's bidding is what comes first.

Among the working dogs whose role is primarily to guard property and people are included the Boxer, the Bullmastiff, the Dobermann, and the German Shepherd Dog (more commonly known as the Alsatian). These are all strong, active dogs with highly developed protective instincts. Although this quality is one of their main virtues, it must not be allowed to develop to the extent that the dog becomes overprotective and aggressive. Difficult behaviour in such large and potentially dangerous dogs can be a real problem, and ownership of such

breeds must be carefully considered, with correct training and handling adhered to at all times. It is vital that dogs such as these are fully aware of their place in the 'pack' and respond quickly and consistently to commands from their owner.

The intelligent German Shepherd Dog is one of several working dogs that is so versatile that it can be employed in a variety of different roles. As its name suggests, it was initially bred as a watchful herding dog, but has found favour the world

over in roles that include police dog, sniffer dog (for drugs, explosives and people buried under collapsed buildings), guard dog and guide dog for the blind. It is also used by the military. Moreover, it is one of the most popular pet dogs of all time.

Keen, alert, responsive, hard-working and intelligent – these are some of the attributes that have made the Border Collie such a successful working dog.

ALASKAN MALAMUTE

This large dog originating in Alaska is named after a local Inuit tribe. The Alaskan Malamute was bred for pulling sleds for long distances over the frozen terrain of Alaska and northern Canada. In fact, it is the largest of all the sled dogs. The breed was brought to the polar regions with the first peoples to settle the land. It was first shown outside its native country in the 1920s.

This is a powerfully-built, handsome dog. The head is broad, with a skull that narrows towards the eyes. The muzzle is large and the nose is usually black, although in red-and-white examples it is brown. The almond-shaped eyes are usually brown; darker shades are preferred, except in red-and-white dogs, when they may be lighter. The ears are small and triangular and are normally held erect but may also be held close to the skull. The strong neck is carried on a deep-chested and powerfully-built body with strong loins. The legs are well-muscled and strong. The tail may hang down at rest but is usually carried curled loosely over the back when on the move.

The Alaskan Malamute has a thick, coarse outercoat and a dense, oily and woolly undercoat. Colours range from solid white, grey through to black, and from gold through red shades to liver; the underbody, legs, feet and mask are always white.

Although strong, the dog is not especially fast. It needs plenty of exercise and has the power to pull enormous weights for long distances – therefore it can also take some stopping if it has a mind to the contrary. Quite a friendly animal, although not necessarily with other dogs, the Alaskan Malamute

The Alaskan Malamute is not the first dog that springs to mind when looking for a pet. It is a handsome and friendly dog with a huge amount of stamina, which means that it requires plenty of regular exercise.

should receive careful training from an early age to ensure it is always under control. It makes an excellent guard dog.

46

ANATOLIAN SHEPHERD DOG

This is a large herding and guard dog much prized by Anatolian shepherds in Turkey. The breed was developed over many centuries from mastiffs that had long existed in the Middle East and the Babylonian Empire. The dog is also known as the Karabash – a reference to its most familiar markings of cream and fawn with a black mask and ears.

They are a tall, powerfully-built dog of the mastiff type. The head has a large, broad skull and a strong muzzle, square in outline. The nose is black. The rather small eyes are golden or brown and are set well apart. The triangular ears are also rather small, compared with the size of the head, and pendent. A powerful, moderate-length neck is carried on a long body with a deep chest and a level back. The legs are long and well-boned. The long tail is carried low and slightly curled when at rest, but is carried curled over the back when the dog is alert.

The outercoat is close-lying and flat, being short and dense with a thick undercoat; the hair on the neck, shoulders and tail is slightly thicker. All colours from cream to fawn are acceptable, with a black mask and ears.

The Anatolian Shepherd Dog is a large, active, alert and intelligent dog. It was bred to guard, and that is what it does best. The breed is extremely hardy but needs a large amount of food to keep its great bulk satisfied. It likes exercise, but is more inclined to move at a leisurely pace.

The Anatolian Shepherd Dog comes from Turkey where it was highly prized for guarding flocks; it still retains this protective instinct. It is a large dog which requires a firm hand, a good deal of feeding, and plenty of exercise.

AUSTRALIAN CATTLE DOG

A tough breed developed to control cattle on long journeys to market, the Australian Cattle Dog is also known by other names, including the Blue Heeler and the Australian Heeler – 'Heeler' being a reference to the dog's habit of nipping the heels of cattle when manoeuvring them. The breed was developed initially by crossings involving sheepdogs, the Dingo, the Kelpie, the Dalmatian and the Bulldog. The breed, which has been pure since the 1890s, is a fairly recent arrival in Britain and the United States.

This is a compact, tough and symmetrical-looking dog with a typical sheep-herding dog's head. The head is

wedge-shaped with a broad skull and a medium-length muzzle. The nose is black. The brown eyes are alert and intelligent. The ears are broad at the base, pricked and pointed. The neck is very strong and muscular. The body has a deep, broad chest and is carried on strong legs. The tail resembles that of a fox.

The coat has a hard, straight, weather-resistant outercoat; the undercoat is short and dense. Colours are blue, blue-mottled or blue-speckled with tan, blue or black markings; or red-speckled with red markings.

Watchful and intelligent, the Australian Cattle Dog loves to work, being tireless and capable of fast movement. Loyal and easy to tame, the breed is wary of strangers.

The Australian Cattle Dog was initially bred to guide cattle over long distances to auction. As a result, it has incredible stamina and is able to work all day. It can be kept as a pet, provided it is given plenty of exercise.

49

AUSTRALIAN SHEPHERD DOG

Despite its name, the Australian Shepherd Dog did not in fact originate in Australia. Its roots lie with the sheepdogs of the Basque region of Spain, and when Basque shepherds emigrated to Australia with their flocks in the 19th century they took some of their dogs with them. Later, these people and their dogs moved again, this time to the United States, which is where the dogs got their name.

This is a long-bodied, well-balanced dog. The head has a squarish and slightly domed skull and the muzzle is slightly tapering towards the nose. The nose is variously coloured; it is black in blacks and blue merles and liver or brown in reds and red merles. The oval-shaped, moderately-sized eyes are blue, amber or brown, or a combination with flecks and marbling. The triangular ears are set high on the head. The neck is of moderate length and is carried on a strong, deep-chested body with a level

back. The legs are of medium length. The tail is straight and may be docked.

The coat is straight or wavy and of medium length and texture; the undercoat is weatherproof. Colours are black, blue merle, red or red merle, all of which may have tan points.

Agile, sure-footed and with well-developed herding and guarding instincts, the Australian Shepherd is nevertheless friendly – although sometimes initially reserved – and quick to learn.

The Australian Shepherd is most likely of Spanish origin, brought to Australia when Basque shepherds emigrated to that country with their flocks of Merino sheep. It has not long been recognized as a separate breed.

BEARDED COLLIE

It is possible that the origins of the Bearded Collie go back to the 16th century, when Polish Lowland Sheepdogs, brought to Scotland by visiting sailors, were bred with local herding dogs. Today, this is one of the most popular and instantly recognizable

of all the breeds, with a strong following both within the farming community and with people who simply appreciate the dog's rascally good looks and appealing nature.

A long-coated, lean and active dog. The head has a broad, flat skull and a fairly long muzzle. The nose is usually black, but may be of a colour harmonizing with the coat in blues or

THIS PAGE & PAGES 52 & 53: The Bearded Collie is a hardy breed with few genetic weaknesses. It needs daily grooming to keep loose hairs and matting at bay, but most think the extra care is well worthwhile.

browns. The eyes also harmonize with the coat colour, and should be large, expressive and friendly. The ears are moderately large and hang down. The slightly arched neck is carried on a deep-chested body with strong loins. The legs are well-boned and muscular. The long tail is normally carried low, with a slight upward curl at the end, but is extended when on the move.

The Bearded Collie's outercoat is flat, strong and shaggy and the undercoat is soft and close; the coat should be long enough to enhance the shape of the dog and to form the characteristic beard. Colours are slate-grey, reddish-fawn, black, all shades of grey, brown and sand, with or without white markings.

An active, self-confident and fun-loving dog with an endearing expression, the Bearded Collie is many people's idea of the perfect pet – although it also makes a highly capable working dog. It is blessed with plenty of stamina and enjoys nothing more than a romp in the open air. The long coat is likely to pick up plenty of the countryside, however, so a thorough grooming is needed to keep it in good condition.

The Beauceron is France's most popular sheepdog, but makes an excellent family pet. As with all herding dogs, it requires plenty of exercise.

The Beauceron's coat is smooth and flat, with fringes on the flanks, legs and tail. Colours are black, black-and-tan, fawn, fawn with dark tips, grey, or grey with black spots.

This intelligent and attractive dog is a good worker and is also good-natured, making it a suitable pet for a family home. As expected from a dog with a long history of herding, the Beauceron is also loyal and protective. It welcomes plenty of exercise.

BEAUCERON

A breed of French origin, this is one of the best-known sheepdogs in France. It was originally used for hunting wild boar, but was later used for sheep-herding and guarding. The Beauceron is also known by its alternative names of Bas Rouge (meaning 'red stocking' – a reference to the tan markings on the legs) and Berger de Beauce.

A lean and muscular dog with a resemblance to the Dobermann. The head is long, the slightly-domed skull and long muzzle being approximately equal in length. The nose is black. The eyes are dark, and should tone with the colour of the coat. The ears may be cropped, or if natural are folded and hang down. The neck is moderately-long, the body being long and deep-chested. The legs are strong and of medium length; the hind legs have double dew claws. The tail is long, unlike the docked Dobermann tail.

BELGIAN SHEPHERD DOG

The Belgian Shepherd has a history stretching back to the Middle Ages, but in the 1890s the breed was differentiated into three separate coat types and four coat colour patterns. The basic body shape of each of these types remains the same, however. Each of the four types of Belgian Shepherd is named after a region in Belgium. These are the Groenendael, the Tervueren, the Malinois and the Laekenois. All of these dogs are sheepdogs and guards, but they are increasingly seen as pet dogs, too.

A medium to large, well balanced and square dog, carrying itself elegantly and proudly; some types are slightly reminiscent of the German Shepherd. The head is fairly long, the skull and muzzle being almost equal in length; the muzzle tapers towards the nose, which is black. The brown eyes are almond-shaped, of medium size, and have a direct, quizzical look. The ears are triangular, stiff and erect. The neck is well-muscled and broad at the shoulders. The body is deep-chested and powerful; the rump slopes slightly. The legs are well-boned and muscular. The tail is long.

The Belgian Shepherd Dog may have three different kinds of coat:

Groenendael: Outercoat long, straight and abundant and fairly harsh; undercoat dense; hair particularly long around neck forming a ruff; fringe of long hair on back of fore legs; hair also long on tail and hindquarters; hair longer on males than on females. Colour is black, or black with small amounts of white on chest and parts of the feet.

Tervueren: Coat similar to that of the Groenendael in length and texture. Colours are red, fawn or grey, with black tipping, this feature being especially apparent on shoulders, back and ribs.

The Belgian Shepherd's handsome exterior conceals a reliable and adaptable animal, fiercely loyal and protective of its family.

Malinois: Coat thick and close; undercoat woolly; hair especially short on head, ears and lower legs; short on rest of body but thicker on tail and around neck; fringing on parts of legs. Colours similar to the Tervueren's.

Laekenois: Coat is hard and wiry but not actually curled; about 2.5in (6cm) in length. Colour is reddish-fawn with black shading, especially on the muzzle and tail.

BERGAMASCO

This herding and guard dog hails from Italy, where it has been used to guard livestock in the mountains in the north of the country for centuries. Its distinctive cord-like coat may have helped to protect it against wolves. The breed became generally more well-known following its success at dog shows in the late 1940s.

The Bergamasco is a heavily- and uniquely-coated sheepdog of medium size. The head has a broad skull, which is slightly convex between the ears; the muzzle tapers slightly towards the nose. The eyes are large and oval; usually chestnut, they impart an alert but calm expression. The ears are triangular in shape and semi-drooping. The neck is strong and is carried on a body with a broad, straight back. The legs are well-muscled. The tail is carried high when on the move but held low and slightly curled at the tip at other times.

Having the appearance of long, matted strands, the long and abundant

coat is hard at the front of the body but softer on the head and legs; the undercoat is thick and oily. Colours are solid grey or all shades of grey up to black.

A solid, strong dog with a highly protective instinct, the Bergamasco is fairly cautious by nature but is also intelligent and vigilant. The coat needs careful grooming.

The Bergamasco came from the mountains of northern Italy, where it was bred to protect sheep from wolves. It has an unusual corded coat which requires a good deal of attention to maintain it in good condition.

BERNESE MOUNTAIN DOG

It is likely that the foundations for this large, affable dog arose from crossings of local Swiss herding dogs and a type of guard dog brought by invading Roman armies into what is now Switzerland about 2,000 years ago. A powerful animal, the Bernese Mountain Dog has long been used to pull small carts loaded with produce to market. The dog gets its name from the Swiss canton of Berne. A popular dog in Europe, the breed is less common elsewhere, although its friendly nature will always win it admirers.

A stocky, well balanced dog with an attractive coat. The head has a broad skull and a medium-sized

muzzle. The almond-shaped eyes are dark brown and kindly. The ears are medium-sized and triangular. A strong and muscular neck is carried on a compact body with a deep chest and a strong, level back. The legs are strongly boned and well- muscled. The bushy tail is raised when on the move.

A long, soft and silky coat; a slight wave is allowed, but the coat should not be curly. The colour is jet black with russet-brown or tan markings. A white blaze is present on the head and a white cross on the chest; white paws and a white tail-tip are desirable.

The Bernese Mountain Dog is delightful and well-mannered, being good-natured and responsive to training. It makes the perfect companion for a country-dweller. The dog has an easy-going view of life and should be encouraged to exercise regularly so as to avoid becoming overweight.

The handsome Bernese Mountain Dog is the perfect pet for the country-dweller, being in its element rambling across hill and dale. Plenty of living space is also required for this very large dog.

BORDER COLLIE

Recognized the world over as one of the finest and most intelligent of all sheepdogs, the Border Collie was formerly used in the regions bordering England, Scotland and Wales, but is now found far and wide. The breed was well-established by the mid 19th century, and a comprehensive stud book and registration system has been in operation in Britain for many years. However, the breed was only registered by the Kennel Club in 1976, since when the dog has featured widely in the show ring as well as in obedience trials. This agile and clever dog has also been used to great effect in rescue work and as a sniffer dog.

A graceful, well-balanced dog with a low-slung body. The head has a fairly broad skull and a moderately short, straight muzzle tapering to the nose. The nose is usually black but may be brown, chocolate or slate to harmonize with other coat colours. The oval eyes are brown, but in merles one or both eyes may be blue; the eyes have an alert and intelligent expression. The ears are medium-sized and are carried semi-erect or erect. The strong, slightly-arched neck is carried on a long, athletic-looking body with a deep chest. The medium-length legs are strong and muscular.

The tail is moderately long and held raised when on the move; it is never carried over the back.

The outercoat is moderately long, dense and medium-textured and the undercoat is soft and dense. Various colours are possible, and these include black, black-and-white, and tan-and-white.

Keen, alert, responsive, hard-working and intelligent – qualities that have made the Border Collie such a successful working dog. It is also loyal and faithful, and responds well to commands. But as a pet these very attributes mean that it can become destructive and difficult if deprived of exercise for both body and mind.

The Border Collie is ever-alert and ready for anything. It is an intelligent, active dog with boundless energy, and requires a corresponding amount of exercise and mental stimulation.

BOUVIER DES FLANDRES

The Bouvier des Flandres was originally bred for herding and protecting cattle in Belgium and also France. In fact, the name translates as 'Flanders Ox-driver'. After the First World War, during which time the dog was also used as an ambulance dog and messenger, the breed was rescued from near-extinction by a Belgian army vet who saved one dog. Today, this big, amiable breed has also found favour as a house pet as well as being used for police work.

A strongly-built and powerful dog with a large head and a compact body.

The head has a flat, wide skull and a broad, powerful muzzle. The nose is black. The oval eyes should be as dark as possible and have an intelligent expression. The ears are triangular. The neck is strong and thickens towards the shoulders. The body is short, deep and strong. The legs are strong, well-muscled and of medium length. The tail is usually docked.

A coarse, rugged and thick coat about 2.5in (6cm) long; the undercoat is dense; the hair around the mouth should form a thick beard, and with the prominent eyebrows gives the dog a somewhat fearsome expression.

Colours range from fawn to black, including brindle; there may be a white star on the chest.

The large Bouvier des Flandres may have a rather forbidding appearance, but it is in fact good-natured, calm and trustworthy, while at the same time being an alert and effective guard dog. Only moderate exercise is required, and the dog settles well into family life.

The Bouvier des Flandres is good-natured despite its slightly forbidding appearance. Given a moderate amount of exercise and plenty of attention, it adapts well to its role as family pet.

BOXER

The likely ancestors of the Boxer are the Bulldog and the Great Dane. A German breed, the Boxer has existed in the form seen today for over 100 years. The breed became unpopular during the First World War, but its popularity was later restored – no doubt due mainly to its virtues as a guard dog and active companion. In America and Germany, Boxers have cropped ears, but in Britain they are left uncropped.

Clean and hard in appearance, the Boxer is a squarely-built and active dog. The head is short and square, with the skin forming wrinkles. The muzzle is broad and deep, with the lower jaw undershot and curving slightly upward. The nose is black. The dark-brown eyes face well forward and impart a lively and alert expression. The ears are set widely apart at the top of the skull and lie flat to the cheeks when at rest, falling forward when alert; ears may be cropped and erect in some countries. The neck is round and strong. The body is short and deep-chested with a strong, slightly-sloping but straight back. The muscular legs are moderately long and terminate in cat-like feet. The tail is usually docked.

The Boxer's coat is short, hard and glossy. Colours are shades of fawn or brindle, with white.

The Boxer needs firm handling and an energetic owner, but it will reward you by guarding your your children and your property with its life.

Extrovert by nature, the Boxer is fearless and confident. Although loyal to family and friends, it can be wary of strangers and therefore makes an efficient guard dog. The Boxer needs firm handling by its owner to remind it who is in charge – especially when in the presence of other dogs towards whom it has a tendency to become rather unfriendly.

BRIARD

There is a legend that a type of dog similar in appearance to the modern Briard helped trace the murderer of the nobleman, Aubry de Montdidier, leading the breed to become known as the 'Chien d'Aubry'. But a more likely explanation may be that the breed hails from the province of Brie, in France. Undoubtedly, the Briard has long been used all over France for sheep herding and guard duties, and has also found employment as a pack dog for the army. Nowadays, the dog is also kept as a rumbustious but friendly pet.

Muscular and well-proportioned, with a long, flowing coat. The head has a slightly rounded skull and a square, strong muzzle. The nose is black. The large, dark-brown eyes have a gentle and intelligent expression. The ears are fairly short and should not hang too close to the head. The neck is moderately long and arched. The deep-chested body has a firm and level back and is carried on strongly boned, well-

muscled legs. The tail is long with an upward curl at the tip.

The Briard has a long and slightly wavy outercoat and a dense undercoat; the head sports a beard, moustache, and eyebrows that form a veil over the eyes. Colours are black, slate-grey or various shades of fawn.

The Briard has an effortless gait and seems to glide over the ground. A friendly and extrovert dog, and good with children, it can on occasions become a little over-boisterous during play. This is a dog that likes plenty of exercise.

A long history of association with human beings as shepherds and pack dogs has made this gentle giant reliable and good-natured. The Briard is fond of boisterous games and is good with children.

BULLMASTIFF

The Bullmastiff came about as a result of crossings between the Bulldog and the Old English Mastiff. The dog was used as a very effective guard dog and gamekeeper's dog – in fact, it was often known as 'the gamekeeper's dog'. A strong animal, but highly amenable to training and correct handling, the Bullmastiff was officially recognized as a breed in 1924, although it had been in existence well before that date.

This is a powerful and symmetrical dog with a smooth coat. The head has a square skull and a deep, strong muzzle. The skin on the head becomes wrinkled

when the dog is aroused. The eyes are hazel or darker in colour and of medium size. Ears are V-shaped and folded, accentuating the square look of the skull. The neck is very muscular and almost as wide as the skull. The body is short with a broad chest and a straight back and is carried on moderately long, powerful legs. The tail is long and tapering.

The Bullmastiff has a short and hard coat that lies flat to the body. Colours may be any shade of brindle, fawn or red.

Powerful and purposeful, and with an independent nature, the Bullmastiff is not a dog for the novice. But it is reliable, faithful and affectionate, and makes an excellent guard dog. It also has the ability to cover the ground with remarkable speed and agility for a dog of such a commanding size and build.

The Bullmastiff is a large and powerful animal, unsuitable for the novice dog-handler. But it is faithful and reliable and makes an effective guard dog.

ROUGH COLLIE

Essentially the same breed as the Smooth Collie, the Rough Collie stemmed from the dark-coated herding dogs of Scotland, which in turn may have had their origins when dogs brought to Scotland by the Romans were mated with local dogs. The Rough Collie achieved royal recognition when Queen Victoria kept the breed at Balmoral Castle in Scotland. Although this form of the breed is today more likely to be seen in the show ring than working on the hills with sheep, it nevertheless retains many of its herding instincts. The breed found immortal fame in the guise of *Lassie*, the famous film star dog.

An attractively coated, well-proportioned dog, the wedge-shaped head has a flat and fairly wide skull and a long muzzle. The nose is black. The eyes are medium-sized and almond-shaped and should impart a gentle expression; eye-colour is dark brown, except in blue merle-coated dogs when they are blue or blue-flecked. The ears are held back when resting, but when the dog is alert they are brought forward and held semi-erect. The neck is powerful and arched, and is carried on a rather long body with a deep chest. The legs are strongly boned and terminate in oval feet. The long tail is held low at rest but held raised when on the move, although never over the back.

The Rough Collie has a very dense, outercoat that is straight and harsh; the undercoat is soft and close; mane and

frill are very abundant. Colours are sable-and-white, tricolour, or blue merle; all colours also include white.

This elegant and beautiful dog makes an ideal pet, being friendly and loyal especially towards its owner. The coat needs plenty of grooming to retain its luxurious appearance.

The Rough Collie or 'Lassie' dog has been popular as a pet for a good many years. However, its spectacular coat must never be neglected so that mats are allowed to form.

SMOOTH COLLIE

This breed is essentially a short-coated version of the Rough Collie, and also comes from Scotland. The same colour varieties are available. Many consider this to be the more attractive and practical breed of the two.

A dog of dignified appearance, giving the impression of ability in the field. The wedge-shaped head has a flat and fairly wide skull and a long muzzle.

The nose is black. The eyes are medium-sized and almond-shaped, producing a gentle expression; eye-colour is dark brown, except in blue merle-coated dogs when they are blue or blue-flecked. The ears are held back when resting, but when the dog is alert they are brought forward and held semi-erect. The neck is powerful and arched, and is carried on a rather long body with a deep chest. The legs are

strongly boned and terminate in oval feet. The long tail is held low at rest but raised when on the move, although never over the back.

The outercoat is short, flat and harsh; the undercoat is dense. Colours are sable-and-white, tricolour, or blue merle; all colours may also include white.

This elegant dog makes an ideal pet, being friendly and loyal especially towards its owner. More of a working dog than its close relative, the Rough Collie, this breed expects more exercise.

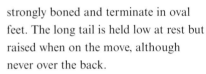

The handsome Smooth Collie is more of a workdog than its rough-coated relative. However, it makes a loyal and friendly pet that requires plenty of regular exercise.

DOBERMANN

The breed takes its name from Herr Louis Dobermann, a German tax collector who bred the dog in the 1870s. He crossed a variety of dogs, including German Shepherd, Pinscher, Rottweiler and Manchester Terrier to produce an animal capable of protecting him – and also of encouraging recalcitrant debtors to pay up! Given its pedigree, it is not surprising that the Dobermann reflects many virtues, including speed, strength and intelligence. In America, where the breed is extremely popular, it is usually referred to as the Dobermann Pinscher.

The Dobermann is muscular and elegant with a smooth, glossy coat. The head has a fairly narrow, flat skull with a rather long, deep muzzle. The nose is solid black in black dogs, dark brown in brown dogs, dark grey in blue individuals and light brown in fawn dogs. The eyes are fairly deep-set and should convey a lively and intelligent expression. The neat ears may be erect or dropped; in some countries they are docked. A long and lean neck is carried on a deep-chested body with a short, firm back. The legs are long and well-boned and terminate in cat-like feet. The tail is usually docked.

The coat is smooth, short and close-lying. Colours are black, blue, brown or fawn, with tan markings above the eyes, on the muzzle, throat, chest, legs, feet and tail.

Unfortunately, the Dobermann has suffered an image problem in the past, being seen primarily as a rather fierce guard dog. However, the breed can make a highly intelligent, loyal and delightful pet for owners willing to train it carefully from puppyhood and to be firm and consistent in handling the dog, so that it knows who is in charge. Careful selection has largely

The Dobermann is an elegant breed, combining a muscular frame with a short, glossy coat. It has acquired a bad image in the past, no doubt because of the common perception that it is a fierce guard dog. With early and careful training, however, it can make a good pet.

reduced the propensity for wayward and bad-tempered behaviour often seen previously. The dog requires plenty of exercise but is easy to groom after a romp in the countryside.

ESKIMO DOG

This tough dog originated in Greenland, although it is often described as coming from Canada, because Canadians were instrumental in the breed's development. Similar in appearance to both the Siberian Husky and the Alaskan Malamute, the Eskimo Dog was bred to haul loads across the frozen northern wastes for the local Inuit peoples as well as for Arctic exploration teams before mechanized transport took over.

Ability has always been more important than temperament with this dog, and unlike many other breeds, the Eskimo Dog has not had a long history of life spent in households among people. Ownership of such a dog – lively, characterful and affectionate though it may be – should therefore not be considered lightly.

A powerful husky-type dog. The head is broad and wedge-shaped with a flat skull and a medium-length, gently tapering muzzle. The nose may be black

With its boundless energy and huge appetite, the Eskimo Dog is not the ideal pet for everyone. However, it is good-natured, intelligent, and enjoys human company.

or brown. The eyes are dark brown or tawny and set rather obliquely, conveying a fearless expression. The short ears are set well apart and held erect. The neck is short and muscular. The strong, well-muscled body has a deep chest and a level back and is carried on heavily-boned legs. The tail is carried curled over the back.

The breed has a thick, double coat. The undercoat is about 1–2in (2.5–5cm) thick and covers the whole body uniformly; an outercoat of coarse, longer hairs protrudes and is longest on the neck, withers, breeches and underside of the tail; fur between the toes helps to protect the feet.

The Eskimo Dog is fairly wary by nature, and early socialization with other dogs is essential. It is also likely to display many of the other characteristics for which it was so highly prized in its homeland, particularly an inexhaustible level of energy and the desire to pull something along – more often than not its owner. It also has a voracious appetite. On the plus side, the breed is generally good-natured, intelligent and enjoys company.

ESTRELA MOUNTAIN DOG

The huge Estrela Mountain Dog comes from the Estrela region of central Portugal where it has long been used for both guarding and herding livestock. A relatively rare breed in many places outside its native homeland, the dog's good-natured character should see it winning over plenty of converts. The breed exists in two distinct coat types: a long-coated and a short-coated form.

A sturdy, mastiff-type dog, the head is long and strong with a broad, slightly-domed skull. The muzzle is slightly tapering and the nose is black. Medium-sized, amber, oval eyes convey an impression of calm. The ears are smallish, triangular and carried at the sides of the head. The neck is short and thick, sitting on a body with a broad, muscular back, a deep chest, and slightly arched loins. The legs are well-boned and well-muscled. The tail is long and well-furred.

The two coat types are as follows:
Long-coated: The outercoat is thick, close-lying and fairly harsh, and may be flat or slightly wavy; the undercoat is dense.
Short-coated: The coat is thick, short, fairly harsh and straight with a short, dense undercoat. Colours are fawn, brindle, or wolf-grey.

A large dog that is remarkably well disposed towards its friends and family, although it can be rather stubborn on occasions. Easy to groom and undemanding in its feeding habits, the Estrela Mountain Dog makes a good companion and guard dog for an active family.

The Estrela Mountain Dog is a sociable animal and enjoys the company of its human family, but it can be obstinate on occasions.

FINNISH LAPHUND

A spitz-type dog from the Nordic countries, the Finnish Laphund was bred to herd reindeer – a task in which it is still involved, in addition to working with sheep and other livestock.

This is a handsome, medium-sized dog with a full coat. The head has a moderately broad skull and a medium to long, wedge-shaped muzzle. The nose is black. The eyes are dark brown, with a confident, intelligent expression. The ears are of medium size and held erect. A strong neck is carried on a long body with a straight, broad back. Strong, medium-length legs terminate in well-arched, oval feet. The tail is carried curled over the back when the dog is on the move.

The Finnish Laphund makes a good household pet in that it is not too large and requires only moderate feeding and exercise.

The Laphund's outercoat is long and coarse, with an undercoat that is dense, woolly and soft. All colours are permitted, with shades of colour differing from the main one appearing on the head, neck, chest, legs and tail-tip.

This is an attractive dog, not too big for the average household and with a responsive nature. The profuse, luxuriant coat needs regular grooming, but the dog is not demanding in terms of feeding or exercise.

GERMAN SHEPHERD DOG

One of the most popular and instantly recognizable dogs wherever it is seen, the German Shepherd is synonymous with excellence and versatility throughout the canine world. Bred to the standard seen today in the later part of the 19th century by German army officer, Max von Stephanitz, the breed was originally used as a sheep-herding dog. Later, however, it found favour as a police and military dog. Indeed, during the First World War nearly 50,000 were used by the German army.

By 1926 it was the most popular dog in Britain, where it was often called the Alsatian Wolf Dog, the term 'Alsatian' being still often used to describe the breed. Poor breeding and thoughtless handling – coupled with the dog's widespread use as a guard dog – unfortunately resulted in it gaining a reputation for aggressive and unpredictable behaviour. The best examples of the breed, however, cannot be praised too highly. Today, the German Shepherd excels in its various roles, including police and military work, tracking, leading the blind, guarding, drug detection, and of course being a perfect companion for an owner prepared to offer the kind of life this intelligent dog deserves.

DOGS

An alert, long-bodied and purposeful-looking dog, the head has a moderately-broad skull and a long muzzle. The eyes are almond-shaped, usually brown, and should convey intelligence and confidence. The ears are medium-sized, broad at the base, and carried erect. The neck is long, strong and muscular. The deep-chested body is long with a straight back that slopes towards the hindquarters; the body-length should be slightly greater than the dog's height. The legs are strong and muscular. The tail is long and bushy and hangs in a curve when the dog is at rest.

The German Shepherd's outercoat is close, straight, hard and weather-resistant; the undercoat is thick, woolly and close. Colours include black, black-and-tan, and sable; occasionally white or cream dogs appear, also long-coated varieties which are not generally accepted for show purposes.

A good-quality German Shepherd makes a highly trainable, tireless, intelligent and loyal companion that is also excellent in a variety of working roles. The dog has supple movements, using a long-reaching gait. It needs plenty of exercise to keep body and mind occupied, although there is a tendency to be lazy if given the chance.

It seems as though the versatile German Shepherd can be trained to do almost any job,

GIANT SCHNAUZER

This is the biggest of the three Schnauzer breeds, and it was used in Bavaria in Germany as long ago as the 15th century for herding duties. It started to become redundant in this role when railways became a more economical option for moving cattle about. However, the Giant Schnauzer's impressive size and appearance meant that it soon found favour in the cities of Germany as a guard dog. For a time, it was known as the Munich Schnauzer. The breed is now popular both as a guarding companion dog and as a police dog.

This is a powerful, long-legged and almost square-shaped dog. The head has a fairly broad skull and a long, strong muzzle. The nose is black. The eyes are oval and dark. The V-shaped ears drop forward to the temple. The strong neck is slightly arched and is carried on a body with a broad, deep chest and a strong, straight back. The legs are long and well-boned. The tail is customarily docked.

The Giant Schnauzer has an outercoat that is hard and wiry, and there should be a good undercoat. The dog has a prominent beard, moustache and eyebrows. Colours are pure black or pepper-and-salt.

As its name suggests, the Giant Schnauzer is the largest of the Schnauzer family, the others being the Standard and the Miniature. It is a powerful dog with an amiable personality and makes an imposing guard dog.

An intelligent, strong, and active dog that is also friendly and reliable. Its size and boldness, however, mean that it can also act as a very effective deterrent to a would-be burglar. The coat needs stripping twice-yearly.

GREAT DANE

Despite its name, the Great Dane is of German origin and not Danish. In fact, it has been the national dog of Germany since 1876. Originally used to hunt wild boar, the breed was initially classed as a hound, and it undoubtedly has hound blood – possibly Greyhound – in its makeup. Another misconception is that the Great Dane is an aggressive dog when it is in fact the archetypal gentle giant.

The Great Dane is muscular, elegant and of imposing appearance. The head has a flattish skull and a deep, broad muzzle. The eyes are round, medium-sized and dark in colour; in harlequins odd, or wall eyes are permissible. The ears are triangular and folded forward; in some countries,

such as America, they are docked. The neck is long and arched and held well up. The body is deep, with slightly arched loins. The legs are long and muscular and terminate in cat-like feet. The long tail tapers towards the tip.

The coat is short, dense and glossy. Colours are brindles, fawns, blues, black, or harlequin (pure white background with black patches or blue patches that appear ragged at the edges).

The majestic Great Dane, despite its great size, is the archetypal gentle giant. However, its great size may exclude it as a pet, which is a pity, as it is patient, loyal and affectionate.

Majestic-looking and with a dignified and friendly nature, the Great Dane is suitable only for those with space and budget to accommodate the dog and its appetite. Devoted to its family, it has an endearing character but sadly a relatively short lifespan.

HOVAWART

Originating in the Black Forest region of Bavaria in Germany, the name Hovawart means 'farmyard warden', and dogs of this type were known to guard farms as far back as the 1200s. Only seen in Britain since about the mid 1970s and in America since the 1980s, the breed was first recognized by the German Kennel Club in 1936.

A medium-sized dog with a strong physique, the head is fairly long with a broad skull and a gently-tapering muzzle. Nose-colour should match the coat. The eyes are oval, have an alert expression, and should be as dark as possible. The ears are triangular and pendent. The neck is of medium length, carried on a moderately-long body. The legs are strong and muscular. The tail is long and bushy, carried high when on the move.

The dog has a medium-length coat, shorter on the face and front legs; the undercoat is fine and light. Colours are black-and-gold, blond, or black.

The Hovawart is a playful dog and is usually devoted to its family. But it can nevertheless become domineering where other dogs are concerned. Easy to feed and groom, and with a good nose for hunting, the Hovawart is a good choice whenever an all-round companion dog is required.

Hovawarts are playful dogs and enjoy family life. But they can be difficult with other dogs and need to be ruled with a firm hand.

HUNGARIAN KUVASZ

Used by Hungarian tribesmen for guarding duties, the Hungarian Kuvasz probably arrived in about 1200, via Turkey. It bears a resemblance to both the Maremma Sheepdog and also to the Pyrenean Mountain Dog, with which it may have a common ancestry. The Kuvasz is quite popular in America.

This is a large, sturdy and powerful dog. The head has a long, slightly arched skull and a broad, slightly tapering muzzle. The eyes are almond-

shaped, dark brown, and set widely apart. The ears are V-shaped and folded. The neck is long and muscular and is carried on a fairly long, deep body. The dog stands on powerful legs, and the hind feet are longer than the fore. The tail is carried level with the loins when on the move, with a slight upward curve at the tip.

The outercoat is slightly wavy, being of a medium to coarse texture; the undercoat is woolly and fine. The coat-colour is pure white.

This is an attractive dog that is by no means one of the easiest to keep as a pet. Although the Kuvasz is gentle and loyal towards those it knows, it is a dog that was bred to guard, and still considers guarding an important part of its life. It is therefore wary of strangers and likes to have a place which it can patrol and guard. The Kuvasz is also big and burly and has a demanding appetite.

The large Hungarian Kuvasz has been bred predominantly as a guard dog. However, it finds it difficult to forget the fact and may take the task too seriously. Though gentle and loyal with those it knows, it is not the ideal pet.

HUNGARIAN PULI

The origins of the Hungarian Puli are not entirely clear, but it is thought that it may have come from Asia in the 9th century. This highly distinctive-looking dog is a herder of sheep, and its unusual corded coat is designed to keep out wet and cold weather.

The Puli is a sturdy, wiry dog, whose body is obscured by its long corded coat. The head has a round skull and a short muzzle, and the nose is black. The dark-brown eyes have a lively expression. The ears are V-shaped and pendent but are scarcely discernible beneath the hair on the

head. The medium-length neck is carried on a body with a broad, deep chest. The legs are strong and muscular. The tail is curled tightly over the rump.

The Hungarian Puli has a thick, long coat that forms into cords as the dog matures, and which is usually longest on the hindquarters; in some individuals the coat reaches the ground. Colours are black, rusty-black, white, grey or apricot.

A lively, alert and highly active dog, the Puli is affectionate with those it knows but naturally wary of strangers, normally greeting them with animated bouts of barking. Despite its appearance, the coat requires plenty of regular attention to keep it in good condition.

As a sheep herder, the Puli's distinctive corded coat is designed to keep out driving wind and rain. Generally longest on the hindquarters, the coats in some cases will actually grow to touch the ground.

KELPIE

This Australian breed came about in the latter half of the 19th century, when imported English collies were mated with local breeds. The dog was first shown in 1908. The Kelpie is used on the vast Australian sheep stations.

The Kelpie is a tough and muscular little sheepdog with a fox-like face. The head has a flat skull and a slightly-tapering muzzle. The brown eyes convey a lively and intelligent expression, and the ears are large, wide at the base and held erect. The powerful neck is carried on a body that is slightly longer than the height of the dog; the chest is broad. The strong legs are of medium length, ending in cat-

like feet. The bushy tail is usually carried low.

The Kelpie has a double coat with a thick, dense undercoat and a hard straight outer coat. Colours are black, black-and-tan, red, red-and-tan, fawn, smoke-blue or chocolate.

The dog is a tireless worker in its native country, where its tough constitution, weatherproof coat, and keen senses make it a highly-regarded sheepdog.

The Kelpie is a tireless worker on the vast sheep stations of Australia. Extreme toughness and a waterproof coat is therefore required to enable the dog to function in all weathers.

KOMONDOR

Another of the cord-coated breeds, this guardian dog resembles the Hungarian Puli although it is somewhat larger. Long known in its native Hungary, the Komondor was probably introduced into the country by wandering Magyar peoples. The coat helps the dog blend in with the flocks of sheep which it guards.

A big, muscular dog, the head has a broad, arched skull and a broad, deep muzzle. The nose is black. The eyes should be as dark as possible and not too deeply set. The ears are medium-sized, U-shaped, and pendent. The strong neck is carried on a body with a deep, muscular chest. The legs are strongly boned and muscular. The tail is slightly curved at the tip and is raised to the horizontal position when the dog is excited.

The dog has a long, coarse outercoat and a soft undercoat; hair forms tassels giving the corded appearance; it may take two years for

the coat to grow to its full length. The colour is always white.

Despite its unusual and disreputable-looking coat, the Komondor is an imposing and effective guard dog with powerful jaws. This is an animal bred for living in the countryside and as such is not really suitable for town life. The Komondor makes a devoted companion, but caring for its coat can be extremely demanding.

The Komondor is an imposing guard dog with powerful jaws, and not entirely suited to family life. Its thick coat also requires a good deal of attention, despite its scruffy appearance.

MAREMMA SHEEPDOG

The dog is used to guard flocks and property in its native Italy. The breed's exact origins are unknown, but it is possible that the dog is a descendant of those owned by the wandering Magyar peoples. The temperament of examples seen outside Italy is reported to have improved considerably over the years.

The Maremma is a large, muscular dog with a thick white coat. The skull is wide between the ears but narrows towards the eyes, and the muzzle is fairly long and tapers slightly towards the nose – the whole head being slightly conical in shape. The nose is black, and

the eyes are almond-shaped and dark brown in colour. The V-shaped ears hang flat to the sides of the head but move forward when the dog is alert. A strong neck is carried on a fairly long, broad body with a deep chest. The medium-length, large-boned legs end in large, almost round feet. The long tail is carried almost level with the back when the dog is on the move.

The waterproof coat consists of a harsh white, ivory or pale-fawn outercoat, with no waviness, and a thick and dense undercoat.

Despite its size, the Maremma Sheepdog is capable of moving easily over rough terrain and of turning quickly. Intelligent and brave, although not aggressive, the breed is rather aloof and naturally wary of strangers but makes a good guarding companion when properly trained.

The Maremma, despite its large size, is very agile, making it capable of moving easily over rough ground. It is not aggressive and its intelligence and courage make it a good guard dog.

MASTIFF

This huge breed is one of the oldest in Britain. Dogs similar in appearance to the modern Mastiff were to be found in Britain at the time of the Roman invasion, fighting alongside their masters as they tried to repel the invaders. Later, recognizing the breed's great strength, courage and presence, the Romans took Mastiffs back to Rome to take part in gladiatorial contests against animals such as bulls, lions and bears. The dog's popularity went into decline in Britain after the Second World War but was revived using imported stock. The Mastiff is also known as the Old English Mastiff.

A massive, powerfully-built dog with a large, heavily-jowled head. The

head has a square skull, a short, broad muzzle, and a marked stop. The small eyes are set widely apart, are brown in colour, and convey an expression of calm and strength. The ears are small and thin and hang down by the sides of the head. The neck is highly muscular. The body has a deep, wide chest and a very muscular back and loins. The legs are large-boned and muscular. The tail tapers at the tip and is held slightly curved when the dog is on the move.

The Mastiff has a short coat. Colours are apricot-fawn, silver-fawn, fawn or fawn brindle.

Fortunately, this large and impressive dog is docile and good-natured, but it still makes an admirable guard dog. It is affectionate and loyal and needs plenty of human company and reasonable amounts of exercise. The Mastiff also has a prodigious appetite – as befits a dog of this size – and this should be taken into account when ownership is being considered.

Despite its imposing size, the Mastiff is a quiet and docile animal that thrives on human company and regular exercise. It also has a voracious appetite which must be taken into account when considering it as a pet.

NEAPOLITAN MASTIFF

The Neapolitan Mastiff is another very ancient breed, thought to be a descendant of the Molossus dogs of Greco-Roman antiquity. Because of its huge strength and size, the dog was once used for fighting, also finding favour as a guard dog and for pulling carts. The Italian writer, Piero Scanziani, established a kennel for the breed and is credited with its revival and promotion; the dog was first shown in 1946. In its native land, the Neapolitan Mastiff is sometimes seen with cropped ears.

A muscular, powerfully-built dog with a massive head. The head has a wide skull and a short, square and deep muzzle. The fairly large, chestnut-brown or black eyes have a penetrating look. The ears are short with triangular tips and usually hang down, although in some countries they are cropped. The neck is short and massive. The body has a broad, muscular chest and is fairly short and deep. The legs are powerful and well-boned. The tail tapers towards the tip; it may be docked by one-third of its length.

The dog has a short, dense and fine coat, with a glossy sheen. Colours are black (preferably), blue, grey and shades of browns.

The dog's gait can be described as bear-like, in that it lumbers along at a slow trot, rarely breaking into a gallop. Reliable, obedient, and not aggressive unless provoked or commanded to attack, the breed is nevertheless not a good choice for the novice owner. The breed's loose jowls and pendulous lips

The Neapolitan Mastiff is an ancient breed with ancestors dating back to ancient Greece and Rome. It is bred to be a guard dog, but is only aggressive on command. Not for the novice dog-handler, however.

mean that it is somewhat inclined to slobber and dribble.

NEWFOUNDLAND

The exact origins of the Newfoundland are somewhat obscure, but it is possible that the breed developed from a type of dog that was brought by nomadic peoples into the northern polar regions and was not actually from Newfoundland itself. From there, the breed was taken by sailors and traders to England, where it became extremely popular.

A large-boned, strong-looking dog. The head is broad and massive with a short, square muzzle. The dark-brown eyes are small and deep-set. The ears are also small and fall close to the sides

of the head. A strong neck is carried on a deep-chested body with muscular loins. The legs are of moderate length and strongly boned, terminating in webbed feet – an invaluable aid to swimming. The tail is of medium length.

The Newfoundland has an oily, waterproof, double coat that is flat and dense. Colours are black, brown (chocolate or bronze), or landseer, i.e. white with black markings, named after the artist, Sir Edwin Landseer, who painted the breed on many occasions.

The name Newfoundland invariably springs to mind when one thinks of dogs and water, since no other breed has such a natural affinity

with the element. Used for centuries to help fishermen retrieve their nets, the Newfoundland also has a deserved reputation as a powerful swimmer and life-saver. On land, the nautical theme is continued, for the dog moves along with a slightly rolling gait. Resembling a cuddly teddy bear, especially in puppyhood, the Newfoundland matures into a delightful character; it is affectionate, docile and willing to please, but is also more than capable of guarding the home.

Newfoundlands and water go hand-in-hand together, and they have for centuries been fishermen's companions. They are powerful swimmers and renowned for saving lives.

NORWEGIAN BUHUND

A spitz breed, the Norwegian Buhund is a herding and guardian dog. The word Buhund means 'the dog found on the homestead', and it was only officially recognized in the early part of the 20th century.

A lightly-built but compact dog, the head is wedge-shaped, with a flat skull and a tapering muzzle. The nose is black. The eyes are dark brown, suggesting alertness and fearlessness. The tall ears are held erect and are very mobile. A medium-length neck is carried on a short, strong body with a deep chest. The medium-length legs are lean and strong. The tail is short and thick and is carried curled over the back in typical spitz fashion.

The outercoat is hard and smooth with a soft, woolly undercoat. Colours are wheaten, red, black, or wolf-sable.

The Norwegian Buhund is a relatively new breed that makes a good family pet, but tends to be wary where strangers are concerned.

Lively and alert, the Norwegian Buhund is a little reserved with strangers but always friendly towards its family. It does not have a big appetite and its coat is easy to groom and keep clean.

OLD ENGLISH SHEEPDOG

Another of the almost universally recognized breeds of dog, the Old English Sheepdog, or Bobtail as it is also known, probably originated from crossings between European and British sheepdogs over 150 years ago. The breed's coat is its most distinctive feature – indeed, there is little else of the actual dog to be seen unless the coat has been clipped. The Old English Sheepdog seems to have made the transition from working dog to highly popular pet and advertising icon, perhaps to the detriment of the breed's original type.

This is a strong, symmetrical and squarely-built dog. The head has a rather square skull and a strong, square muzzle. The nose is black. The eyes may be dark or wall-eyed; sometimes the eyes are blue. The ears are small and carried close to the sides of the head. The neck is fairly long and arched. The short, compact body with muscular loins is carried on long, strongly-boned legs. The tail is usually completely docked.

Hard-textured and profuse, the outercoat should be free from curl but shaggy, with a waterproof undercoat. Colours are grey, grizzle or blue in any

shade; the head, neck, forequarters and under-belly should be white, with or without markings.

Cheerful and extroverted, the Old English Sheepdog is always ready for action. It is a breed that needs plenty of exercise, and careful, regular grooming is required if the coat is not to become hopelessly matted. The dog walks with a bear-like gait but moves freely and effortlessly at speed.

Plenty of time and patience is needed if you have an Old English Sheepdog as a pet. Its coarse, longhaired coat needs very regular attention, while the dog itself, having been bred for hard work, needs a good deal of exercise.

PINSCHER

This is a clean-looking, medium-sized dog of German origin, with an appearance reminiscent of a small Dobermann. Recognized by the German Kennel Club in 1879, the dog is also known as the Standard Pinscher, the word 'pinscher' meaning 'terrier', although this dog is too long-legged to go to earth, as does the typical terrier. Instead, it is used for other tasks, for example, as a watchdog.

This is a smooth-coated, elegant dog. The head has a moderately wide skull and a deep muzzle. The nose is black. The eyes are oval, dark, and of medium size, and have a lively and intelligent expression. The ears are V-shaped and usually folded, although they are sometimes cropped. The neck is elegant and well-muscled. The body is deep-chested, carried on strong, medium-length legs. The tail is usually docked.

The Pinscher has a short, dense and glossy coat, the colours most commonly seen being black and tan, red, fawn, and blue and tan. A neat and nimble dog, the Pinscher is easy to groom and inexpensive to feed. Obedient, lively and friendly with those it knows, its wariness of strangers makes it a useful guard dog.

The German Pinscher was one of the breeds used by Louis Dobermann to develop the powerful and imposing dog to which he gave his name. The Pinscher itself is somewhat smaller, is nimble and attractive, and makes a rewarding and useful pet.

POLISH LOWLAND SHEEPDOG

With an ancestry that is believed to include the Hungarian Puli and long-coated herding dogs, the Polish Lowland Sheepdog has been in existence since at least the 16th century. Polish sailors visiting British seaports at that time are thought to have exchanged these dogs for native ones, and so helped the breed to spread. The sheepdog became almost extinct after the Second World War, but was saved by the efforts of a Polish vet who, using some of the few remaining animals, ensured the continuance of the breed.

This is a chunky, muscular, long-coated breed reminiscent of the Bearded Collie. The head has a fairly broad, slightly arched skull, with a muzzle that is equal to it in length. The nose should be as dark as possible. The eyes are hazel or brown and have an alert expression. The moderately large drop ears are heart-shaped. The neck is muscular and strong. The body, carried on well-muscled legs, is rectangular when seen from the side, with a level back and muscular loins. The tail is usually docked, although some dogs are born without a tail.

The hard-textured outercoat is long, thick and shaggy; the undercoat is soft. Long hair covers the eyes. Any colours are acceptable.

This is a lively, intelligent and friendly dog that seems particularly fond of playing with children. The Polish Lowland Sheepdog needs plenty of exercise to help burn off some of its exuberant energy, but rewards its owner by being easy to train and happy to act as a dutiful watchdog. The long coat needs careful grooming.

The Polish Lowland Sheepdog is full of exuberance and energy and has a fondness for children. It requires plenty of exercise and regular grooming, but you will be amply rewarded for your trouble.

PORTUGUESE WATER DOG

The dog probably arrived in Portugal with Moorish traders from North Africa. For centuries, the breed's great love of water has been put to good use by Portuguese fishermen, who use the dog for salvaging tackle and nets from the water and for guarding their boats. The dog comes in two different coat types: a long, wavy coat and a shorter, curly coat. The coat is usually clipped short over the hindquarters and most of the tail.

This is a rectangular, muscular dog reminiscent of a Poodle. The head has a long skull and a strong, slightly tapering muzzle. The eyes are round and are dark brown or black in colour. The drop ears are heart-shaped. The neck is short and straight and is carried on a short, deep-chested body. The long legs are well-boned and muscular, ending in webbed feet (an aid to swimming). The tail is long and tapering and is carried in an arch over the back; a plume of hair decorates the tail-tip.

The two coat types are as follows: *Long-coated:* Thick and loosely waved; fairly glossy. *Short-coated:* Harsh and dense with tight curls; not glossy. Coat clipped into the characteristic style. Colours are black, white, brown, black-and-white, or brown-and-white.

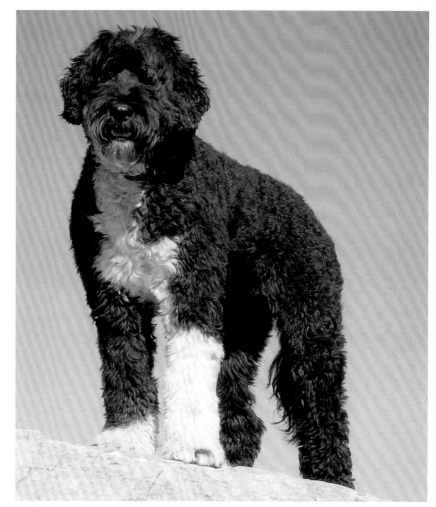

The Portuguese Water Dog is a cheerful, intelligent and energetic animal, with excellent swimming abilities. The breed can be obstinate at times, so firm handling is required.

As its name suggests, the Portuguese Water Dog loves water and has webbed feet to facilitate swimming. It is an intelligent and lively animal, but quite difficult to train, making it unsuitable for the novice owner.

PYRENEAN MOUNTAIN DOG

For centuries, this large and impressive dog was used to guard flocks against wolves, bears and other predators in the French Pyrenees. A descendant of the herding and guardian breeds of southern Europe, the dog was a favourite with French noblemen, and it was named the Royal Dog of France by Louis XIV. During the Second World War, the Pyrenean was used as a pack animal and as a messenger by French troops. Today it is a popular companion dog. It is also known as the Great Pyrenees.

The Pyrenean Mountain Dog is strong, well-balanced and elegant. The

head has a broad, slightly arched skull and a medium-length, slightly tapering muzzle. The nose is black. The almond-shaped eyes have a thoughtful expression and are a dark amber in colour. The ears are triangular, lying against the sides of the head when the dog is resting. The neck is thick and muscular. The chest is broad and deep and the back is broad and muscular. The legs are heavily boned and well-muscled, as befits such a powerful dog; the double dew-claws help the dog to tackle the mountainous terrain. The tail tapers towards the tip and is carried with the tip slightly curled.

The outercoat is fairly long, coarse and thick, and may be straight or wavy; the undercoat is profuse. The coat forms

a mane around the neck and shoulders. Colours are white, or white with patches of badger, wolf-grey, or pale-yellow.

The Pyrenean has a confident, kindly and dignified air, but as with any big dog, correct handling is required. Surprisingly, the breed requires only average amounts of exercise and is likely to amble along rather than take off at speed. The dog makes a good house pet, but its coat needs plenty of care and attention.

The Pyrenean Mountain Dog was originally used to protect flocks of sheep against wolves, but found a new role during the Second World War as a messenger. Today, its role is more usually that of a companion and family pet.

PYRENEAN SHEEPDOG

This much smaller dog from the Pyrenees region of France probably originated from crosses between indigenous Pyrenean breeds and others, such as Briards. It was used for herding flocks of sheep. The breed is a fairly new arrival in Britain, and only received Kennel Club recognition in 1988. The coat may be long or semi-long.

This is a small, active, rough-coated sheepdog. The head has a fairly flat skull and a short, slightly tapering muzzle. The almond-shaped eyes give the dog a keen and active look; they are usually dark brown, although one or both may be blue or blue-flecked in

merle or slate-coloured dogs. The ears are fairly short. The neck is medium to long, and is carried on a lean, strong body with slightly arched loins. The legs are lean but well-muscled; the hind legs may have single or double dew-claws. The tail is medium-length with a slight hook at the tip; the tail may be docked, and some individuals may be born with a stump tail.

The coat is rather hard and dense, and may be flat or wavy. Colours are fawn, light to dark grey, blue merle, slate blue or brindle, black, or black-and-white.

Like many herding breeds, the Pyrenean Sheepdog has plenty of energy and stamina. It likes plenty of exercise but is undemanding when it comes to food. A good watchdog.

The Pyrenean Sheepdog comes from the French side of the mountain range and was probably the result of cross-breeding between indigenous breeds and Briards. Agile and spirited, the dog requires plenty of exercise.

ROTTWEILER

The name of this dog comes from the Roman settlement of Rottweil in Germany. When the Roman Empire was invading Germany, mastiff-type dogs were brought along too, for guarding and herding livestock. In time, Rottweil became an important trading centre for cattle and other livestock, and butchers in the town used the dog for various duties, such as for pulling carts. Today, the breed's natural boldness and guarding instincts have made it popular for use by police forces and other similar organizations. The Rottweiler first appeared in Britain in the 1930s and is one of the most popular dogs in America. Overbreeding produced some poor examples, but this problem has now diminished.

A compact, powerful and well-proportioned dog. The head has a wide, medium-length skull and a deep, broad muzzle. The nose is black. The brown eyes are almond-shaped, and the ears are small and pendent. The neck is strong, round, and very muscular. The body has a broad, deep chest with a strong, straight back. The legs are well-boned and muscular. The tail is normally docked at the first joint.

The Rottweiler has a medium-length outercoat that is coarse and flat; the undercoat should not protrude through the outercoat. Colour is black, with well-defined tan markings on cheeks, muzzle, chest, legs, over the eyes and beneath the tail.

This is a bold, loyal, and courageous dog that is also very active; therefore, it likes plenty of exercise. The short coat responds well to grooming, and a splendid sheen is easily produced. The Rottweiler is a willing worker and an excellent guard dog, but correct handling and training are essential requirements for ownership of such a strong breed.

The Rottweiler has a long history dating back to Roman times. It is a formidable animal and requires careful handling from puppyhood to make it manageable. Not for the faint-hearted.

SAINT BERNARD

It would be difficult to mistake the St Bernard for any other dog, for this gentle giant is depicted everywhere as a symbol of rescue and care. A descendant of mastiff-type dogs brought to the Swiss Alps by the Romans over 2,000 years ago, the dog achieved fame when it was used by the monks at the Hospice of St Bernard for rescuing travellers lost in the St Gothard Pass. There are two coat-types: rough- and smooth-coated.

A well-proportioned, massive dog of substance, the huge head has a broad, slightly rounded skull and a short, deep muzzle. The nose is black. The dark eyes are medium-sized and should have a benevolent expression.

The triangular ears are also medium-sized and lie close to the cheeks. The neck is thick and muscular with a well-developed dewlap. The deep-chested body has a straight back and muscular loins and is carried on straight, heavily-boned legs. The feet are large, which no doubt help the dog progress through snow. The tail is long.

There are two coat-types:
Rough-coated: Flat and dense and full around the neck. *Smooth-coated:* Close-fitting and hound-like with feathering on the thighs and tail. Colours are orange, mahogany-brindle, red-brindle, or white with patches on the body of any of these colours.

Fortunately, this massive dog is an extremely benevolent character with a steady, calm nature. Walks are usually taken at a leisurely pace, but a St Bernard can pull extremely hard, so needs to be kept under control. The dog is inclined to drool and is not one of those large breeds that can curl up into surprisingly small spaces; indeed, owners tend to fit themselves into whatever space is left over. Feeding is an expensive undertaking.

The St Bernard has a placid, affectionate nature, but because of its massive size and strength requires careful handling.

SAMOYED

The Samoyed was originally used to guard the reindeer herds and pull the sleds of the wandering tribesmen of the Siberian tundra. Fur traders brought the breed back to Britain. Samoyeds have also been used on a number of polar expeditions.

A well-proportioned and graceful spitz-type dog, with a sparkling, stand-off coat. The head is wedge-shaped with a wide skull and a medium-length muzzle. The nose may be black, brown or flesh-coloured. The brown eyes are almond-shaped, enhancing the 'laughing' expression so characteristic of this dog. The ears are thick with slightly rounded tips, and are held erect. The strong neck is carried on a broad, muscular body with a deep chest. The legs are very muscular and well-boned. The tail is held curled over the back and to one side.

The Samoyed has a thick, close, short undercoat and a harsh, straight outercoat which grows away from the

body, giving protection from the cold. Colours are pure white, white-and-biscuit, and cream.

A charming dog that loves human company. Fairly obedient in a rather laid-back way, the breed nevertheless enjoys life and lets everyone know it. The coat needs plenty of grooming, but the Samoyed is quite happy to submit itself to any amount of attention.

The Samoyed is a lively, jolly animal, fairly obedient despite having a mind of its own. The thick coat can be rather troublesome to the dog in warmer climates, however, and very regular grooming is required.

SHETLAND SHEEPDOG

The bleak Shetland Islands, off the north-eastern coast of Scotland, are the original home of this small dog, which bears a strong resemblance to the Rough Collie. Although small, the breed was quite capable of working with Shetland ponies and other livestock of the area.

An elegant and symmetrical dog, the head is in the shape of a blunt wedge, the skull being flat, fairly broad, and with a long, rounded muzzle. The nose is black. The almond-shaped eyes are obliquely set and are usually dark brown, although they may be blue or blue-flecked in merles. The small ears are usually carried semi-erect with the

tips falling forward. The well-arched neck is carried on a deep-chested body with a level back. The muscular legs are moderately long. The tail is well-furred.

The Shetland Sheepdog's outercoat of long hair is hard and straight; the undercoat is soft and short. Hair forms an abundant mane and frill over neck and shoulders. Colours are sable, tricolour, blue merle, black-and-white, and black-and-tan.

This attractive little dog makes a good companion for people of all ages, being watchful, intelligent and energetic. The breed has undemanding feeding requirements, but the luxuriant coat does require a good deal of careful grooming.

The Sheltie has brains as well as beauty and, like the Shetland pony, has been bred small. Although there is a resemblance, it is not a miniaturized Rough Collie.

SIBERIAN HUSKY

The Siberian Husky was developed by the Chukchi peoples of Arctic north-east Asia as a fast, long-distance sled dog. Indeed, this is the fastest of all the sled-pulling breeds, and the dog seems happiest when performing this task. Although more lightly built than other sled dogs, the Siberian Husky is tough, strong and full of endurance.

This is a purposeful, medium-sized dog. The head is rather fox-like in appearance, with a slightly rounded skull and a medium-length muzzle. The nose is black in grey, black or tan dogs, liver in copper-coloured dogs, and flesh-coloured in white individuals. The eyes are almond-shaped and may be brown, blue, or parti-coloured. The triangular ears are held firmly erect. The neck is arched and is carried on a medium-length muscular and deep-chested body. Well-muscled, powerful legs end in oval, slightly webbed feet with fur between the toes. The tail has a fox-like brush.

The outercoat is straight and smooth-lying; the undercoat is soft and

dense. The coat may be of any colour, including white.

Friendly and extremely tolerant towards human beings, the same cannot always be said about the Siberian Husky's attitude to other dogs, which it will usually try to dominate. Indifferent to the coldest of weather, the breed is not a typical pet by any means. It will jump over almost anything, or dig under it, and will usually pull on the leash and then take off when released. The breed is mostly kept for sled racing.

The Siberian Husky is not the ideal pet, and will jump over fences and dig its way out of anywhere. It can also be agressive with other dogs and because of its dense coat is not very happy kept indoors, having been bred to work outside in a harsher climate.

SWEDISH VALLHUND

Looking very much like a Welsh Corgi, the Swedish Vallhund – also called the Swedish Cattle Dog – was rescued from near-extinction in the 1930s. The Swedish Kennel Club recognized the breed in 1948. The dog was bred to help herd cattle by nipping at their heels, thereby encouraging them to move along.

This is a low-slung, sturdy little dog. The head is shaped like a blunt wedge, with a flat skull and a squarish muzzle. The nose is black. The oval eyes are dark brown in colour. The ears are pricked and mobile. The neck is long and strong, carried on a deep-chested body with a strong, level back. The legs are fairly short, well-boned and muscular. The natural tail is 4-in

(10-cm) long, but puppies may have their tails docked.

The outercoat is medium-length, hard, and close-fitting; the undercoat is thick and woolly. Colours are steel-grey, grey-brown, yellow-grey, reddish-yellow or reddish-brown.

A cheerful, obedient and active dog, the Swedish Vallhund makes a good family pet; both feeding and grooming are undemanding.

Similar in appearance to the Welsh Corgi, the Swedish Vallhund makes an undemanding pet, in that it has a moderate appetite and a low-maintenance coat.

TIBETAN MASTIFF

For centuries, the breed has been used in the foothills of the Himalayas for guarding flocks of livestock from marauding predators and for guarding people's homes.

The Tibetan Mastiff is a massive, powerfully-built yet dignified dog. The head is large, with a wide skull and a short, square muzzle. The oval eyes are very expressive and may be any shade of brown. The ears are triangular and pendent and hang close to the head. The neck is strong and muscular. The deep-chested body is strong, with a straight back. The sturdy, muscular legs terminate in large cat-like feet. The longish tail is held curled back over one side of the body.

The outercoat is quite long, thick and fine, with a heavy undercoat; hair forms a thick mane on the head and

shoulders. Colours are black, black-and-tan, brown, and shades of gold, grey and blue.

Slow to mature (it takes about four years for a male to become fully adult), the breed is fairly aloof with strangers, but friendly and attached to its owner. Essentially a large breed of guard dog, and one that enjoys exercise, the Tibetan Mastiff needs firm handling.

Being wary of strangers, the Tibetan Mastiff makes a formidable guard dog, while at the same time being much attached to its owner. It requires firm handling and plenty of exercise.

WELSH CORGI (CARDIGAN)

Originally bred as a cattle dog, the Cardigan Welsh Corgi is the older of the two varieties of Welsh Corgi, with a history going back 800 years. Even so, it is the least known of the two breeds, and the only one with a tail. The Cardigan differs from the Pembroke in other respects, too, such as in coat-colour, ear-length and foot-shape.

A sturdy, short-legged and active dog, the head has a fox-like appearance with a wide, flat skull and a tapering muzzle. The nose is black. The eyes have an alert but kindly expression and should be dark, although one or both may be blue or blue-flecked in merles. The ears are proportionately large with rounded tips, being widely-spaced and held erect. A muscular neck is carried on a long, fairly broad-chested body. The legs are short but strong, and the feet are round. The brush-like tail is long enough to touch the ground but is usually lifted when on the move.

The coat is weatherproof, being short or slightly longer and with a hard texture. Any colours are permitted.

Active and fast-moving on occasions, the Cardigan Welsh Corgi can also take life at a steadier pace when it has a mind. Intelligent and obedient, the breed makes a good companion and watchdog.

Not to be confused with the Pembroke Corgi (overleaf), the Cardigan Corgi is a much older breed and differs in several respects, having larger ears and a brush-like tail. Both make rewarding pets.

WELSH CORGI (PEMBROKE)

The better-known of the two breeds of Welsh Corgi, this version usually has its tail docked. Another cattle-driving dog, the Pembroke also earned its keep by nipping at the heels of cattle to encourage them to move on – a trick that on occasions has been tried on human beings as well! Besides having a long working history, the dog is a favourite pet of Queen Elizabeth II of England, who has owned many examples of the breed over the years.

A sturdy, short-legged and active dog, the head has a fox-like appearance, with a wide, flat skull and a tapering

muzzle. The nose is black. The round eyes are brown in colour, and the ears are of medium size with rounded tips, widely-spaced and held erect. A fairly long, muscular neck is carried on a long, fairly broad-chested body. The legs are short but strong, and the feet are oval. The tail is usually docked.

The weatherproof coat is short or slightly longer and has a hard texture. Colours are red, sable, fawn, or black-and-tan, usually with white markings on the legs, neck, chest and face.

A popular and outgoing dog, the Pembroke makes a good companion for an active family, liking nothing better than a good romp out in the open air, followed by a good square meal. Its fondness for food, however, should be moderated to avoid obesity.

The Pembroke Corgi's chief claim to fame is its popularity with the British Royal Family, since the breed has been kept for many years by Queen Elizabeth and her mother before her.

98

Chapter Two
TERRIERS

The word 'terrier' comes from *terra*, the Latin word for earth, and aptly describes the part of the landscape in which these dogs were originally employed, having been bred to drive badgers, foxes, rabbits and other quarry from their underground retreats. On occasions, when the terrier could not reach into the burrow or earth, it would still indicate the presence of the quarry to the hunter, who would then unearth it using other means.

Because of the qualities required to perform these underground tasks, most terriers are small to medium-sized dogs, often with short legs, great digging skills, and powerful jaws – but always with huge amounts of courage and tenacity. In time, the name terrier also came to be applied to dogs that were kept for despatching vermin, such as rats and mice.

Because different sorts of terriers were required for working over many varied kinds of terrain, cross-breeding with other types of dogs became common practice. Thus terriers required

to keep up with huntsmen on horseback might be bred with hounds to improve their stamina and increase the length of their legs, while those used for fighting would be bred with mastiffs and other large, powerful dogs to improve their skill in combat. Many of these new terrier breeds arose because of local needs, and often bear the names of the places where they originated, examples being the Manchester, Skye, and Australian Terriers.

The rise in the popularity of terriers began in the latter part of the 19th century, when dog shows exposed many of these animals to a wider audience, and it was also the period when many of the breed standards were set. As with many other dog breeds, shows today tend to concentrate on appearance, and terriers have consistently been among the top award-winners around the world.

Terriers range in size from the largest, the Airedale Terrier (which is 24in /61cm at the shoulder), to the much smaller Norfolk Terrier (standing at only 10in/25.5cm). Despite these great differences in size, terriers usually display many shared characteristics, being naturally alert and curious dogs, sharp in movement and with an ancestry that dictates a fondness for going to ground. They also have a great propensity for digging – much to the alarm and consternation of owners with well-kept gardens.

On the whole, terriers are robust dogs, and being less sensitive than many other pedigree breeds, make good pets for young growing families. Being of a more compact size, they do not object to being picked up and cuddled by young children, are always ready for action and for joining in with childrens' games, and don't take it too personally when scolded for doing wrong. They can, however, be a little too ready to pick fights with other dogs they may encounter along the way, tending occasionally to charge straight in without prior warning.

About two-thirds of the world's terrier breeds originated in Britain. Some breeds of terrier are not classed in the main terrier group, but are placed with others, such as the toy dogs or the utility group. Furthermore, the so-called Tibetan Terrier is not a terrier at all, being related to the working dogs.

The coats of some of the terrier breeds require regular clipping or trimming – often referred to as stripping – to retain their classic,

OPPOSITE: This Lakeland Terrier puppy is so endearingly mischievous that even its naughty ways are soon forgiven.

BELOW: The Norwich Terrier is a tough, active little dog, being one of the smallest of the working terriers.

strong-lined appearance. This is usually carried out professionally twice-yearly, although for show purposes more detailed preparation is usually required.

AIREDALE TERRIER

This breed, the largest by far of all the terriers (and sometimes called the King of Terriers for this reason), originated in Yorkshire, England. The dog reflects both terrier and hound ancestry in its makeup and behaviour, although it is too big to go underground in the traditional way of terriers. The Airedale's imposing size means that, among other duties, it is used on occasions as a guard dog.

The Airedale is a muscular, cobby and active-looking dog. The head is long and flat, and not too broad between the ears, and the nose is black. The dark eyes usually have a lively expression. The V-shaped ears are small, folded, and placed high at the sides of the head. The neck is muscular and is carried on a body with a short, strong and level back; the chest is deep. The legs are long and well-boned. The tail is strong and carried high; the dog is customarily docked.

The texture of the outercoat is hard, wiry and dense, with a softer undercoat. Colour is tan, with a black or grizzle saddle, top of neck and top of tail.

The dog's remarkable scenting ability means that it is used for tracking, for detecting victims in collapsed buildings, and for hunting game. It also comes into its own as an intelligent and courageous guard dog, while at the same time being a devoted and protective family dog, always ready to join in the next game or simply act as a faithful companion. Not a huge eater, despite its size, it is nevertheless a dog with a healthy appetite.

The Airedale is the largest of the terriers, originally developed to hunt otters, badgers and wolves. It is a lively and adaptable dog which should be handled firmly but kindly so that it will learn to accept that it is not the one in control.

AUSTRALIAN TERRIER

Thought to have been bred from British terriers imported into Australia by early settlers, the Australian Terrier achieved show recognition in Britain in 1936. This is one of very few terrier breeds to have originated outside Britain.

This is a low-set, longish dog, with a rough coat and a 'ready-for-action' demeanour. The head is long with a flat skull and a longish muzzle. The nose is black, the dark-brown eyes being small and keen-looking. The small ears

are pricked and devoid of long hair. The neck is long and slightly arched. The body is quite long, given the dog's height, and is fairly deep-chested. The legs are quite short, and the tail is docked.

The coat is long, straight, and hard to the touch. There are two colours: the coat may be blue, steel blue or dark blue-grey with tan on the face, ears, underbody, lower legs and feet. The topknot is blue or silver. Alternatively the coat may be sandy or red, with the topknot in a lighter shade.

A bright, lively little dog with a hardy constitution, the breed likes plenty of exercise and play and, being anxious to please, makes a cheerful and affectionate pet.

The Australian Terrier's talents as a catcher of rats and snakes may no longer be to the fore, but it still retains all the characteristic pluckiness associated with the working terrier.

BEDLINGTON TERRIER

A dog with one of the longest traceable pedigrees of any terrier, the Bedlington hails from Rothbury in north-east England; indeed, its original name was the Rothbury Terrier. The high-arched back suggests there is some Whippet blood in its ancestry, among other breeds. Originally a dog bred with the intention of catching food, such as rabbits for the pot, the breed remains a tough and spirited performer despite its lamb-like appearance.

A graceful and muscular dog with a large, wedge-shaped head. The skull is narrow, deep and rounded, and the eyes are small, bright and triangular, the colour varying with the coat colour. The ears are moderately long and hang flat to the cheeks. The neck is long and tapering and is carried on a long, muscular body with a deep chest and arched back and loins. The legs are moderately long, ending in hare-like feet. The tail is long and tapering and is never held over the back.

The thick coat, with its characteristic texture, is described as 'linty', and has a tendency to twist on the head and face. Usually trimmed to produce the appearance so distinctive of the breed, the coat can be blue, blue-and-tan, liver or sandy.

The Bedlington's gentle and unusual appearance belies its true terrier nature. It is capable of fast movement, although its characteristic mincing gait is more in evidence at slower speeds. This is a confident and intelligent dog which is also good-natured and affectionate.

Despite its unusual appearance, the Bedlington is far from lamb-like, and retains all the qualities of a champion ratter.

BORDER TERRIER

The Border Terrier originated in the border region between England and Scotland, although the name is probably a reference to the fact that the dog worked with the Border Foxhounds. The present name was adopted in the early part of the 19th century, but the breed was not recognized by the UK Kennel Club until 1920. A true worker, the dog was bred to enter foxes' lairs to flush out its occupants, and there was also the need to keep up with riders on horseback.

This is a tough, no-nonsense little dog with typical terrier attributes. The head is shaped like that of an otter but with a broad skull and a short, strong muzzle. The nose is black, liver, or flesh-coloured. The dark eyes have an alert expression. The ears are small, V-shaped, and folded. The strong neck is carried on a deep, narrow, and fairly long body. The legs are moderately long. The tail is fairly short and carried high, although not over the back.

The outercoat is thick and harsh with a dense undercoat. Colours are

red, wheaten, tan-and-grizzle, or tan-and-blue.

The Border Terrier is as it looks, being a strong, well-boned and active little terrier whose job it is to flush out foxes. Its legs are sufficiently long for it to keep up with horse riders, yet the dog is small enough to be picked up when necessary. It also needs strong jaws and a chest narrow enough for it to move in and out of underground lairs. Despite these workmanlike qualities, the dog also makes a kindly and adaptable family pet.

The Border Terrier has a happy-go-lucky nature, allowing it to adapt happily to family life despite having been bred to work and perform specific tasks.

BULL TERRIER

The Bull Terrier was first bred in Birmingham, England, by crossing dogs with Bulldog and terrier blood with English White Terriers. Standardization of the breed is accredited to James Hinks, and the Bull Terrier Club was formed in 1887. The breed has a unique appearance, but unfortunately has also gained a reputation for its pugnacious

THIS PAGE & PAGES 108 & 109: The Bull Terrier has always been prized for its courage, tenacity and speed. Today, it may be a sweet-natured, gentle and playful pet, but having once been a ferocious fighter, firm and careful handling is needed if it is to co-exist peacefully with other dogs.

behaviour. Today, however, breeders have succeeded in producing an animal with a more sociable attitude towards other dogs. A miniaturized form also exists; this is almost identical in appearance to the standard Bull Terrier, but is only 14in (35.5cm) in height.

This is a muscular, stocky dog with a characteristic egg-shaped head. The long, strong head has powerful jaws and a gently sloping profile from the top of the head down to the nose-tip. The nose is black. The eyes are narrow, triangular and slanting. The ears are small and pricked. The neck is long and muscular. The body has a very broad chest, when viewed from the front, and a short, strong back. The legs are moderately long with strong bones. The tail is short and carried horizontally.

The Bull Terrier has a short, flat, harsh but glossy coat. Colours are pure white, black, brindle, fawn, red or tricolour.

Despite the Bull Terrier's rather intimidating appearance – it stands four-square in a manner not unlike a bull, from which its name is partly derived – it is in fact well-disposed towards human beings. However, it can be rather obstinate on occasions, and needs firm handling to ensure peaceful co-existence with other dogs.

CAIRN TERRIER

The Highlands of Scotland and the Isle of Skye are the original home of the Cairn Terrier, where it was bred for hunting otters, badgers and foxes. No longer required for these duties, the breed nevertheless remains a popular dog for the house. The breed was first shown in 1909, although dogs of this type can be traced back over 500 years.

A game little dog with a wiry, slightly unkempt look, the head is small with a broad skull and a powerful

muzzle. The nose is black. The hazel eyes are deep-set and offset by shaggy eyebrows. The small, pointed ears are pricked. The compact body is strong, with a deep chest and a level back. The legs are short and strongly boned. The tail is short and well-covered with hair.

The Cairn has a thick, harsh outercoat with a short, close undercoat. Colours are cream, red, wheaten, grey, or nearly black – all of these colours may be brindled, while the ears and muzzle may be darker.

An alert and endearingly mischievous-looking dog, the Cairn is fearless and ready for anything. It also makes an affectionate companion, delighted to be out and about with its owner – whether romping in the country or simply walking in town.

The Cairn has contributed elements of its alert and vibrant personality to other terriers through cross-breeding. As a pet, it is delightful and fun-loving and needs only moderate exercise to keep it happy and healthy.

CESKY TERRIER

The Cesky Terrier was bred in the Czech Republic for work underground. So far, the breed is relatively rare outside its country of origin and was only registered in Britain in 1990.

This is a short-legged dog, rather long in the body when compared with its height. The head is fairly long and has a slightly arched skull. The nose is black in blue-grey dogs, liver in brown dogs. The eyes are black or brown depending on the coat-colour. The ears are triangular and hang down. The powerful, medium-length neck is arched. The body is long with a level

back, and there is a slight rise over the loins. The legs are short but muscular. The tail is long and is carried slightly aloft when on the move.

The wavy coat has a silken sheen and is usually clipped, except on the upper part of the head, legs and underbody. Colours are blue-grey or light brown.

Tough, hardy and agile, the Cesky Terrier is a somewhat wary yet nevertheless friendly dog.

Still relatively rare outside the Czech Republic, where it originated, the Cesky Terrier is a tough, short-legged little dog that was bred to go to ground.

DANDIE DINMONT TERRIER

The fictional character Dandie Dinmont, from the novel *Guy Mannering* by Sir Walter Scott, is the inspiration for the name of this breed, although dogs of this type existed in the region bordering England and Scotland long before the story was penned. The dog was originally developed for hunting otters and badgers.

The Dandie has a ferret-like body, short legs, and a large, distinctive head, which has a large, almost square skull and a deep muzzle. The nose is black. The dark hazel eyes are large and expressive, and the ears are pendulous. The strong and muscular neck is carried on a long, deep body with well-arched loins. The legs are short and heavily-boned, the hind legs being a little

longer than those at the front. The tail is short.

The double coat consists of a hard, crisp outercoat and a soft undercoat. The fore legs are feathered, and the head is covered with soft, silky fur. Colours are pepper or mustard.

The Dandie Dinmont is able to work well while at the same time be a devoted and affectionate pet – albeit a rather wilful one on occasions.

Originally bred to work hard for its living, the Dandy Dinmont is today usually a devoted and affectionate pet. Being a terrier, however, it can still be wilful on occasions.

SMOOTH-HAIRED FOX TERRIER

This is one of the most popular and well-established of all terriers. It originated in Britain and has an ancestry that is probably linked with Bull Terriers and Manchester Terriers. The standard for the breed was drawn up in the 1870s. This terrier is a valuable addition to the foxhound pack, being small enough to chase foxes from cover which is too inaccessible to be reached by larger dogs. Although fashionable in the show ring, the breed has remained true to its original type.

A compact and purposeful-looking dog, the skull is flat and rather narrow, and the muzzle is long and strong. The nose is black. The eyes are small and dark with an alert, intelligent expression. The breed has small, V-shaped drop ears. The neck is moderately long, lean and muscular. The body has a deep chest and a short, level back. The legs are quite long and strong. The tail is docked and carried jauntily.

The coat is smooth, short, hard and dense. Preferred colours are all-white, black-and-white, tan-and-white.

Big enough to cope with foxes and strong enough to run with the hunt, the Smooth-Haired Fox Terrier is lively and eager. The breed needs a firm hand but rewards a caring owner with devotion and affection. Not usually one to start an argument with other dogs, this terrier will nevertheless give a good account of itself if provoked.

The Smooth-Haired Fox Terrier was bred to run with the hunt and flush out foxes from spaces too small for larger dogs to enter. This is a lively little dog which makes a rewarding pet while needing a firm hand.

WIREHAIRED FOX TERRIER

It is likely that this terrier was developed before its smooth-haired counterpart, although it was the latter that appeared first in the show ring. The Wirehaired was originally called the Rough-Haired Terrier. A popular family dog, the breed appears at its best when the coat is trimmed into the characteristic classic shape.

A compact and well-balanced dog, the skull is flat, rather narrow and slightly sloping. The muzzle is long and strong, and the nose is black. The eyes are small and dark with an alert, intelligent expression. The small drop ears are V-shaped and moderately thick. The neck is fairly long, lean and muscular. The body has a deep chest and a short, level back. The legs are

strong and muscular. The tail is docked and carried erect.

The outercoat is wiry and dense with an undercoat of shorter, softer hair. Colour is mainly white with black, tan, or black-and-tan markings.

Bred for sporting pursuits, this is yet another big-hearted terrier. Fearless and ever-ready, the breed also makes an excellent family pet, expecting to join in every game and always on guard to ward off intruders.

The Wirehaired Fox Terrier is seen in its best light when the characteristic trim has been carefully maintained. This is especially important if the dog is to be shown.

GLEN OF IMAAL TERRIER

Achieving recognition in 1930, the Glen of Imaal Terrier gets its name from a glen in the Wicklow Mountains, Ireland, where it was developed to dig into fox lairs and badger setts, and where its bowed front legs were considered ideal adaptations for the task. While still uncommon, the breed's good nature and characterful appearance may well serve to increase its appeal.

This is a tough-looking little dog, longish in the body and short of leg. The head has a fairly broad skull and a tapering muzzle. The nose is black, and the brown eyes are quite widely-set and intelligent-looking. The small rose-shaped ears are half pricked when alert but are held back when the dog is at rest. The strong neck is carried on a long body with a broad chest. The legs are short and strongly boned; the front

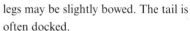

legs may be slightly bowed. The tail is often docked.

The Glen of Imaal Terrier has a medium-length, coarse outercoat with a soft undercoat. Colours are blue, wheaten or brindle.

This terrier, like most of its kind, is alert and active, and is also at home in water. It is gentle and affectionate where people are concerned.

The Glen of Imaal Terrier originated in the Wicklow Mountains of Ireland, where it was used for digging out foxes and badgers. Like most terriers, it is full of pluck and vitality and ready for anything.

IRISH TERRIER

The Irish Terrier, or Irish Red Terrier as it was once called, was first shown in Ireland in the 1870s, although it had been used by sportsmen for many years before that – and indeed still is. This was the first Irish dog breed to be recognized by the British Kennel Club.

The Irish Terrier is a wiry, racy-looking dog with an attractive reddish coat. The head is long with a flat, fairly narrow skull. The nose is black. The eyes are dark and full of life. The drop ears are small and V-shaped. The neck is of a fair length and is carried by a moderately-long body with a straight, strong back; the loins are muscular and

slightly arched. The legs are quite long with plenty of muscle and bone. The tail is usually docked to about three-quarters of its length.

The coat is hard and wiry, with a broken appearance. Colours are red, red-wheaten or yellow-and-red.

The breed has a reputation for being a bit of a daredevil – rushing into action without fear of the consequences. It can also be intolerant of other dogs, but with its human companions it is the very model of devotion, sensitivity, affection and good nature.

The Irish Terrier can be rather impetuous and wilful and as a result can land itself in hot water! It does, however, enjoy family life, and given a firm hand makes an affectionate pet.

KERRY BLUE TERRIER

The Kerry Blue Terrier is believed to have originated in Kerry, Ireland, where it was originally used by farmers for hunting foxes, otters and badgers. Nowadays, with careful trimming to achieve the classic Kerry shape, it has been transformed into a successful show dog. In the 1920s, when the breed reached its peak, there were four clubs in Ireland devoted to the Kerry Blue.

A well-proportioned, muscular and upstanding dog. The long, lean head has strong, deep jaws and a fairly long muzzle. The nose is black. The eyes are small and dark and convey a typically keen terrier expression. The V-shaped drop ears are small. The neck is long and is carried on a short, deep-chested body. The legs are long and powerful, ending in small feet. The tail, customarily docked, is carried erect.

The Kerry Blue Terrier has a profuse, soft and wavy coat. The colour may be any shade of blue. Puppies are born black, and the colour may take up to 18 months to develop.

This is an extrovert and determined dog, bred for an outdoor life. It shows many of the characteristics typical of terriers, being bold and game, and also makes a good pet and house guard. Regular trimming is required to maintain the typical 'look'.

Like most terriers, this is a determined and extrovert breed. The coat must be carefully trimmed to maintain the classic Kerry shape.

LAKELAND TERRIER

The breed was developed in the Lake District of England, its role being to run with the foxhunts. The Kennel Club formerly recognized the breed in 1921. A popular show dog, one Lakeland Terrier achieved Best in Show at Crufts in 1967 before going on to become Best in Show the following year at the American Westminster show.

Regular grooming is needed to maintain the dog's classic appearance.

The Lakeland is an attractive, compact and purposeful-looking dog. The head features a flat skull and a broad, moderately-long muzzle. The nose is black, except in liver-coloured dogs when the nose is also liver. The eyes are hazel or a darker shade. The ears are V-shaped and folded. The neck

is slightly arched and carried on a shortish body with a strong back. The legs are long and powerful. The tail is customarily docked and carried high, but never over the back.

The coat is dense, hard and weatherproof. Colours are black-and-tan, blue-and-tan, wheaten, red, red-grey, liver, blue or black.

Although small, the Lakeland Terrier is a tough, fearless and active dog, ever-alert and ready to work all day if necessary. The breed is also endearingly cheerful and affectionate, and even its occasional naughty ways are soon forgiven.

The Lakeland Terrier was originally bred to run with the hunt, but has excelled itself in the show ring in recent years. It requires regular grooming to maintain its classic appearance.

MANCHESTER TERRIER

Around the mid 1850s, rat-catching contests were extremely popular in Britain, and heavy wagers were placed on the outcome. This breed was developed for just such activities and soon gained the name of Manchester Terrier. The breed combined all the qualities required of such a sporting dog – terrier instincts, a great turn of speed (there is a suggestion of Whippet in its ancestry) and a clean and easy manner in the home.

An attractive, clean-looking and smooth-coated dog, the head is long and wedge-shaped with a long, flat skull. The small, almond-shaped eyes have a special sparkle to them. The small, V-shaped ears are carried above the topline of the head. The longish neck joins a short, narrow body with slightly arched loins. Long and muscular legs end in semi-hare-like feet. The tail is short and tapering.

The coat is short, close and glossy. The colour is jet black and rich mahogany tan; the breed standard calls for very precise placement of the tan markings.

A graceful and elegant breed, the Manchester Terrier is a sporting all-rounder that also enjoys family life.

A graceful and elegant breed, the Manchester Terrier is a highly efficient rodent-catcher and general sporting dog. The breed also makes a devoted family companion, capable of fitting into a town or country home, and is the ideal choice for any owner wanting a breed with a bit of a difference.

NORFOLK TERRIER & NORWICH TERRIER

The Norfolk Terrier, and the almost identical Norwich Terrier, take their names respectively from Norfolk, in England, and its county town of Norwich. The breeds was developed by crossing small red terriers with other terriers. Originally, there was no distinction between the Norfolk and the Norwich, but in 1964 it was decided that dogs with drop ears would be called Norfolk Terriers and dogs with prick ears would be classed as Norwich Terriers. The descriptions which follow apply to both breeds, with the exception of the style of ears already described.

These are small, compact and keen-looking dogs. The head has a broad, slightly-rounded skull. The muzzle is wedge-shaped with a well-defined stop. The oval eyes are deeply-set and either black or dark brown; they should have an alert expression. The ears are medium-sized and

Norfolk and Norwich Terriers are almost identical, apart from the ears, the Norfolk (opposite) being the drop-eared type, while the Norwich (right) has pricked ears. Small and compact, they both make fun-loving pets, like exploring, and are great at digging holes.

pointed; in the Norfolk Terrier they are folded, and in the Norwich Terrier the ears are held erect. A strong, medium-length neck is carried on a short, compact body. The legs are shortish but strong. A docked tail is optional.

The coat is hard, straight and wiry, the hair being slightly longer on the neck and shoulders; the hair on the head and ears is shorter and smoother. Colours are red, wheaten, grizzle or black-and-tan.

These tough, active little dogs have occasionally been used to hunt badgers, foxes and rats. They love to dig and to explore any holes into which they can disappear. Fearless, they make lovable, friendly pets.

PARSON JACK RUSSELL TERRIER

The Parson Jack Russell Terrier gets its name from a Devonshire parson, the Reverend Jack Russell. He was a keen huntsman who bred a small, active terrier using, among others, Fox Terriers. The dog has now achieved show status and comes in either smooth-coated or rough-coated forms. Only a few kennel clubs recognize the Jack Russell, and thus there are no official breed standards. The Parson Jack Russell described here is a longer-legged animal than the short-legged version so commonly seen in farmyards and family homes.

This is a no-nonsense dog resembling a shorter-legged Fox Terrier. The head has a moderately broad and flat skull. The nose is black. Keen, almond-shaped eyes give the dog an alert expression. The ears are V-shaped and folded. The neck is medium-length and muscular and is carried on a body with a strong,

straight back. The legs are strong and muscular. The tail is straight, and is usually docked.

Parson Jack Russells have a hard, dense and close coat in both smooth- and rough-coated varieties. Colours are all-white, or white with tan, lemon or black markings.

A tough, active little worker, the dog has been bred for pace and endurance. It is a playful and intelligent rascal with sharp eyes and sharp wits; it makes a good house pet but can be destructive if left alone long enough to become bored.

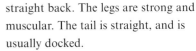

The Parson Jack Russell may be small but it will take up any challenge, and should be kept on a leash when other dogs are around.

SCOTTISH TERRIER

A breed hailing from the Highlands of Scotland, the dog was originally used to destroy rodents and foxes. The standard for the breed was drawn up in 1880, and the Scottish Terrier Club was formed in 1882. Although still fairly popular, the Scottish Terrier is less commonly seen than it was about 50 years ago.

A sturdy, short-legged and thick-set dog, the head gives the impression of being large in comparison with the body, being long and with a flat skull. The dark-brown eyes are deeply set beneath prominent eyebrows. The ears are finely pointed and pricked. A muscular neck is carried on a body with a deep chest and a short, muscular back. Short, strong legs terminate in good-sized feet. The tail is of moderate length and tapers at the tip.

The outercoat is hard, dense and wiry, and the undercoat is short, soft

and dense. Colours are black, wheaten or brindle.

Possibly somewhat reserved at times, the 'Scottie' is nevertheless a vigilant and loyal companion. When ready for a game, it can move remarkably swiftly in pursuit of a toy, such as a ball.

The Scottish Terrier, while it is a loyal companion, is inclined to be stubborn and needs careful handling from an early age to prevent it from dominating the household. It is capable of a good turn of speed, when the mood takes it, and makes an excellent watchdog.

SEALYHAM TERRIER

This breed came about as the result of an obsession to produce 'the perfect terrier'. The person responsible for this undertaking was Captain John Edwardes of Haverfordwest in Pembrokeshire, Wales. Over 150 years ago, he crossed a variety of terriers, including Bull Terriers and West Highland Whites, with Welsh Corgis to produce what became known as the Sealyham Terrier, designed for hunting rats, foxes and badgers. The breed of today is somewhat different from the one envisaged by its original creator, but it remains a versatile and active dog.

This is a mobile, well-balanced dog of substance. The head has a broad, slightly-arched skull and a long, square muzzle. The nose is black. The round eyes are of medium size. The ears are fairly large and folded. A long, thick and muscular neck is carried on a medium-length body with a deep, broad chest. The legs are short and strong and terminate in cat-like feet. The tail is short, customarily docked, and is carried erect.

The Sealyham was the result of an experiment to produce the perfect terrier, which resulted in a versatile little dog that is adaptable to any situation.

The outercoat is hard and wiry with a weather-resistant undercoat. Colours are all-white, or white with brown, lemon, blue or pied markings on ears and head.

This faithful and intelligent little dog is able to make itself at home anywhere. Always ready for play, it can usually find a way of amusing itself during times when its owner is busy.

SKYE TERRIER

Originally called the Terrier of the Western Isles, the Skye Terrier gets its name from the Isle of Skye in Scotland. The dog was bred to hunt animals such as foxes, polecats, martens, otters and badgers. Most of these terriers have prick ears, but there is also a variety with drop ears.

The Skye Terrier is a low, long dog with a very full coat. The head is long with a strong muzzle and a black nose. The eyes are close-set and dark brown to hazel in colour. The ears may be prick or drop and are fringed with hair.

The neck is long, and the legs are short. The tail is long and gracefully feathered.

The highly characteristic outercoat is long, hard and straight, and the undercoat is woolly and soft. Colours are black, also grey, cream or fawn with black points.

This faithful breed tends to become extremely bonded with its owner, but can be wary of strangers. The Skye Terrier makes a good watchdog despite its size. The coat needs regular grooming to keep it free from mud and other detritus.

The Skye Terrier tends to be wary of strangers, a quality which makes it a good watchdog.

SOFT-COATED WHEATEN TERRIER

An old breed of Irish terrier, the Soft-Coated Wheaten Terrier is very similar to the Kerry Blue in appearance and temperament. Indeed, they were both bred to carry out similar duties, i.e. hunting foxes, rats or badgers. The coat may either be trimmed or left natural. The breed was registered with the Kennel Club in Britain in 1943, and with the American Kennel Club in 1973.

A medium-sized, compact terrier with a soft, wheaten-coloured coat, the head is fairly long with a flat-topped skull and there is a well-defined stop. The nose is black. The eyes are dark hazel with dark rims. The drop ears are V-shaped. The neck is moderately long, arched, and muscular. A short and compact body is carried on strong, moderately-long legs. The tail, customarily docked, is carried jauntily but never arched over the back.

The coat is soft and silky, curled or loosely waved, and is especially profuse on the head and legs. Colour should be clearly wheaten.

The Soft-Coated Wheaten is a natural sort of terrier with an extrovert and playful disposition, being ready for action at any time. With patient training the breed makes an excellent pet, and it is particularly good with children.

The Soft-Coated Wheaten Terrier is now rare in Ireland where it originated. It can get along with moderate exercise provided it is regular.

STAFFORDSHIRE BULL TERRIER

The result of crossings between Bulldog and terrier, the Staffordshire Bull Terrier was bred as a fighting dog – used especially to bait bulls and bears in the 19th century; but when this cruel sport was abolished, the dogs were pitted against each other instead. The name 'Staffordshire' comes from the breed's association with England's Black Country, where the breed was developed. Recognized as a true breed only in the 1930s, the dog is popular in the show ring today.

A smooth-coated dog of muscular build and with a low centre of gravity. The head is short and deep with a broad skull and prominent cheeks. The nose is black. The round, medium-sized eyes are usually of a dark colour, but may vary according to coat-colour. The ears are rose-shaped or half-pricked. A short, muscular neck is carried on a body with a broad chest and strong shoulders. The legs are well-boned and set widely apart. The tail is of medium length, carried rather low.

The coat is short, smooth and close-lying. Colours are red, fawn, white, black or blue, or any of these colours with white; also brindle or brindle-and-white.

The breed's reputation as a pugnacious fighter means that it needs careful training and firm handling when in the vicinity of other dogs. With human beings, however, the Staffordshire Bull Terrier is affectionate and calm and is patient with children. The dog is naturally brave, strong, and fiercely tenacious; it also has a lively intelligence.

The Staffordshire Bull Terrier was bred to fight and can be aggressive with other dogs, making careful training and firm control a necessity. With human beings, however, it is a different matter, and the dog is good in the home and patient with children.

WELSH TERRIER

Originally used for hunting badgers, foxes and otters, devotees of the Welsh Terrier say that it looks like a smaller version of the Airedale Terrier (which, in terms of colour, it certainly resembles), although it is more likely that it shares a common ancestry with the Lakeland Terrier. It was introduced to the United States in the 1880s.

A squarely-built, workman-like dog with a smart appearance, the head has a flat, fairly narrow skull and a longish muzzle. The nose is black. The

eyes are small and dark, giving an impression of courage and determination. The drop ears are small and triangular. The neck is long and slightly arched and is carried on a short body with strong loins. The legs are moderately long and well-boned. The tail is docked and carried jauntily.

The coat is profuse, dense and wiry; a double coat is preferred. Colours are black-and-tan, although black, grizzle-and-tan is permitted.

The Welsh Terrier has the typical terrier-like 'tip-toe' stance, suggesting it is alert and ready for anything. A good worker, the breed also makes a clever and happy companion, being far from shy, always affectionate, and usually obedient.

The Welsh Terrier is a lively and cheerful breed, reminiscent of the Airedale. Originally a working dog, it is equally happy living in the home.

WEST HIGHLAND WHITE TERRIER

Originally known as the Poltalloch Terrier, the breed is thought to have originated in Poltalloch, Scotland, where the Malcolm family had been developing these white terriers for several generations. These smart little sporting dogs are not only much admired in the show ring, but also popular as companions and pets.

An eager, squarely-built little terrier, with a characteristic white coat, the head has a slightly arched skull with a tapering muzzle and a black nose. The medium-sized eyes are set widely apart, should be as dark as possible, and look keen and alert. The ears are small, erect and pointed. The body is compact, with a deep chest and broad, strong loins. The legs are short

ABOVE & PAGES 130 & 131: The West Highland White has held its place as one of the most popular breeds for many years. It has a cheeky little face and will never refuse an opportunity for a game.

and strong. The tail should be as straight as possible and carried jauntily aloft.

The outercoat is long and free from curl; the undercoat is short, soft and close. The colour should be pure white.

The 'Westie' is a deservedly popular little dog. Possessing a lively and outgoing personality, it is always ready for a game and seems to be full of boundless energy. A sharp bark to warn off strangers also makes it a useful guard dog

Chapter Three
HOUNDS

The common feature of all the dogs in this group is that they pursue game. If necessary, they then prevent the quarry from escaping, and may bark to pinpoint its location for the hunter before he arrives to despatch it. Being able to corner the quarry in this way was a particularly important requisite before the advent of efficient guns.

Most of the dogs in this group are hounds that hunt by sniffing the ground to pick up and then follow a scent, calling and barking all the while. Dogs of this type include Foxhounds, Beagles and Bassets. The sport of hunting game on horseback – using a pack of hounds to track down the quarry – was a popular pastime in medieval France. There, kings and rich noblemen hunted in the extensive broadleaved forests for foxes, wild boar and deer. Later, following the Norman Conquest, this pursuit was introduced to England.

Keeping packs of hounds became a highly developed activity. Dogs were carefully bred to ensure continuity of

the best strains for working over the terrain and to pursue a particular quarry. Furthermore, specific colours and types were selected in order to produce a uniform appearance throughout the pack. Large hounds with great strength and stamina were used to accompany hunters on horseback, chiefly in pursuit of foxes, deer and wild

boar. In due course, smaller mutations and basset-type hounds were developed; these were used by hunters following on foot to capture smaller game such as badgers, rabbits and hares. The dogs would usually be sent underground to flush the animal out of its lair. For such work, dogs with specific features would be obtained through selective breeding. These features included shorter legs to enable them to tunnel underground and powerful jaws for dealing with the quarry.

The ancestor of the pack hound is the Chien de Saint Hubert. For many centuries it was bred in a monastery in the Ardennes region of Belgium, and until the 1780s the monks there were required to give six hounds to the king each year. Although purebred specimens of the breed ceased to be found any longer in Belgium or France, in England it continued to flourish in the form of the Bloodhound, a breed that was believed to have been brought to England by William the Conqueror. Despite popular belief, the name

DOGS

'bloodhound' does not indicate that the hound can follow a blood trail – although its powers of scent detection are phenomenal – but refers to the fact that the breed has pure blood.

Some hounds hunt primarily by sight, one of the best-known of the sighthounds being the Greyhound. Sighthounds rely on their eyes, rather than their noses, to detect prey before giving chase. Then, the dogs use their enormous speed and power to overtake and despatch the quarry. Typical sighthounds include Salukis, Whippets and Afghan Hounds – all characterized by their long-legged, supple and slender bodies capable of carrying the dog at speed.

There are some hounds that encompass both the virtues of the scenthounds and the sighthounds. They include the Pharaoh Hound and the Ibizan Hound, characterized by their sleek appearance and large, erect ears. Some of these breeds are of very ancient origin; similar-looking animals adorn artefacts found buried in the tombs of the Egyptian pharaohs thousands of years ago, proving that dogs such as these were prized by the rulers of these early civilizations.

Another group of hounds, the spitz dogs, are multipurpose hounds, and includes breeds such as the Elkhound and the Finnish Spitz. Typically, these dogs are large and stocky, with erect ears and bushy, curled tails. Their thick coats help them to keep warm in very cold weather. These large, tough dogs were bred to give chase to game such as wolves, elks and bears in frozen, wooded terrain and then to hold the game at bay, signalling their whereabouts with loud and distinctive calls. Today they are more commonly used for hunting gamebirds.

In addition to their skills as hunters and trackers, many hounds

OPPOSITE: Powerful and agile, the Rhodesian Ridgeback is a loyal and protective dog towards its family. However, it may not be the ideal choice for people unused to keeping dogs.

BELOW: One of the oldest of all British breeds, the impressive-looking Deerhound was developed in the Scottish Highlands, having been brought to the country possibly by Phoenician traders.

make excellent guard dogs, too. They also make friendly, gregarious, affectionate and loyal companions.

AFGHAN HOUND

As its name suggests, this sighthound comes from the mountains and plains of Afghanistan. One of the most glamorous of dogs, with something of a regal air about it, the Afghan is in fact a powerful hunter, and in its native country is also prized as a watchdog and herding dog. The first Afghans arrived in Britain in the early 1900s, and the breed achieved great acclaim at the 1907 Crystal Palace show. Afghans were imported into America in 1926.

Afghans are large and dignified, at the same time giving the impression of power and speed. The head is held proudly. The skull should be long but not too narrow. The nose should be black, although liver is permissible in dogs with lighter-coloured coats. Dark eyes are preferred, but golden-coloured eyes are sometimes found. The almond-shaped eyes slant slightly upwards at the outer corners. The ears are carried close to the head and are covered with long, silky fur. The well-muscled, moderate-length body with deep chest is offset by long, strongly boned legs and a long tail with a ring at the tip.

The coat is long and fine, except on the foreface, and with a silky 'topknot'. Both fore and hind feet should be covered with long fur. All colours are acceptable.

Intelligent and with a distinctly oriental expression, these dogs appear reserved and aloof. However, they are quite capable of playing the fool when the mood takes them. Afghans are also affectionate towards their owners, although they are one of the more demanding breeds to keep. The high-stepping gait and long, flowing coat are characteristics of this breed. Afghans

The elegant Afghan requires a good deal of exercise, but has a natural tendency to chase small animals. It is very attached to its owner, making an excellent pet, even though grooming may be something of a chore.

enjoy plenty of exercise, having a natural tendency to chase small animals, and need regular grooming.

AMERICAN FOXHOUND

The result of crossings between a pack of hounds brought from Britain to Maryland in the United States in 1650, and dogs imported later from countries such as England, France and Ireland, today's distinctive American Foxhound was developed over time. The sport of foxhunting in America differs greatly from foxhunting elsewhere, and the breed reflects those differences.

American Foxhounds are used in field trials and for racing, as well as for foxhunting with guns.

The dog's skull is fairly long and domed and the muzzle is longish with a moderate stop. The large eyes must be brown and should have a gentle expression. The moderately low-set ears should be long and pendulous, and with a fine texture. The deep-chested body with well-sprung ribs is narrower

than in the English Foxhound. The long, strongly boned legs terminate in short feet. The tail is long, held high, and has a slight brush.

American Foxhounds are friendly, non-aggressive dogs, although they can be rather determined and ill-disciplined on occasions. Their natural stamina and endurance stand them in good stead as hunters.

The American Foxhound is a good-natured dog with a wilful side to its nature that requires careful attention.

BASENJI

The Basenji has its origins in what is now called the Democratic Republic of Congo, although dogs similar in appearance to this breed are found throughout central Africa and were even depicted as palace dogs at the time of the pharaohs. The Basenji is still used as a guard dog, companion and hunter in its native land, and is adept at catching rats and other vermin. The first two examples were brought to Britain in 1895, but it was not until 1937 that imports were successfully bred in Britain. The breed was imported to America in 1941. Today, the Basenji has a small but enthusiastic fan club.

A fine-boned and lightly built animal, the Basenji always looks poised, aristocratic and alert. The well-chiselled, wrinkled head narrows towards the point of the nose, which should be black. The dark, almond-shaped eyes have a fixed, somewhat inscrutable expression. The ears are small, pointed and pricked. The neck is well-arched, long and strong. The body is short and deep, with a level back. The tail curls tightly over the back and lies to one side of the thigh in a single or a double curl.

The Basenji's coat is short, smooth and fine. Colours range from black-

and-white, red-and-white, tan-and-white, or black. There should be white present on the feet, chest and tail-tip. White legs, blaze and collar are optional.

Intelligent, curious, and renowned for its cleanliness and lack of odour, the Basenji is an ideal pet that can become very bonded to its family. Basenjis do not bark, but instead make unusual yodelling sounds when they want to express themselves, the wrinkled brow giving them a somewhat quizzical expression. Basenjis love to chew, even when past the puppy stage, so it is a wise precaution to give them plenty of toys to destroy instead.

The Basenji has been known to wash itself like a cat, so fastidious is it about its appearance.

BASSET FAUVE DE BRETAGNE

This little dog came originally from Brittany, France. It is likely that the breed was created by crossing the Griffon Fauve de Bretagne with Brittany Bassets – both hunting breeds of dog. The Basset Fauve de Bretagne is a quite recent introduction into Britain.

This is a neat, nimble animal with a moderately broad and long skull, the fairly long muzzle ending in a slight stop. The nose should be black or at least dark, and the dark eyes should bear a lively expression. The ears are

thin and pendulous. The body is broad, with a fairly deep chest and a level back. The short, muscular legs can be straight or slightly crooked and end in short, strong feet. The tail is long.

The coat is harsh and dense, but not long or woolly. Colours are golden-wheaten, red-wheaten, or fawn. A white spot on the chest is permitted.

Lively, friendly and not too big for even a small home, this dog is gaining popularity as a house pet. Tough and always ready for exercise or play, the breed is easy to groom and feed.

The Basset Fauve de Bretagne, a Breton dog that originated when Brittany was a royal kingdom in France.

BASSET HOUND

The ancestor of the Basset Hound was believed to have been bred for hunting by French monks in the Middle Ages. A close relative of the French Bassets, the breed was nevertheless developed separately in Britain through crossings with Bloodhounds, and was introduced to shows in Britain in 1875. Lighter types of Basset are used as pack dogs when hunting hares, but the heavier ones are used in the show ring and as pets.

A heavily-built, slow-moving and sometimes ponderous dog with a somewhat comical, worried expression. The long, broad head is heavily domed and bears long, pendulous ears. There is loose skin around the head and muzzle. The nose should be black, although it can be brown or liver in lighter-coloured dogs. The eyes are brown or hazel; the red coloration of the lower lids should be visible. The low-slung body is long and with a broad, deep chest and arched loins. Short, heavy legs end in massive feet. When moving, the

LEFT, PAGES 140 & 141: The Basset Hound may look mournful but it is an accommodating animal, as happy ambling through fields and sniffing out prey as it is idling away hours by the fireside.

long and tapering tail is held well up and slightly curving.

The Basset's coat is short and smooth, without being too fine. Usually black, white and tan, any recognized hound colour is acceptable.

Tenacious and full of endurance, this is a dog that loves paddling through wet fields, sniffing out prey, but which is equally at home idling its time away by the fireside with its family. The Basset's deep-chested bark may suggest an unfriendly nature, but this is a false impression, for this amiable dog is good-natured and placid. On the move, the Basset usually proceeds at a steady, lumbering pace, although it can break into a run if required.

BEAGLE

The smallest of the pack hounds, the Beagle is an English breed used for hunting hares, the hunters following on foot. The breed has been in existence since at least the reign of Henry VIII, and is deservedly popular in many countries, including America, Britain and France.

The Beagle is a bustling, active and enthusiastic dog of compact build. The head is medium to broad with a slightly domed skull. The nose should preferably be black. The ears hang down to the cheeks and are thin, fairly long, and rounded. The eyes are brown or hazel, with a friendly look. The medium-length neck is carried on a short, deep-chested body. The strongly boned, muscular legs end in round feet. The tail is moderately long and is carried high.

The coat is dense, short and waterproof, and may be in any of

the recognized hound colours apart from liver.

Bold, lively and affectionate, the Beagle is also blessed with stamina and intelligence. Ever ready for action, it is as happy hunting in a pack as it is simply being a pampered family pet. The short coat is quick to wash and dry, after even the muddiest of romps, but once free of the leash, the dog may take off after a scent trail, seemingly deaf to its owner's calls.

The Beagle's smooth shorthaired coat is easy to maintain and needs little grooming to keep it looking smart.

BLOODHOUND

The origins of the Bloodhound can be traced back to Belgium, where legend has it that the breed was used for hunting in the Ardennes as long ago as the 7th century. The Bloodhound was introduced to England by William the Conqueror in 1066. The name 'bloodhound' has been incorrectly attributed to the dog's legendary ability to follow a blood trail, when in fact it is a reference to 'bloodstock' and the dog's aristocratic breeding.

A huge hound with great presence, the long, narrow head has characteristic hanging folds of pendulous skin, giving a somewhat

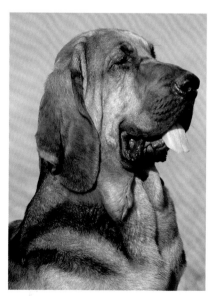

lugubrious expression to the face. Eyes are brown or hazel. The long ears fall in graceful folds and feel soft to the touch. A long, throaty neck is carried on a short, deep-chested body. Long, muscular legs contribute to the dog's imposing size. The long, thick tail is carried high when on the move.

Bloodhounds have smooth, short, waterproof coats. Colours are black-and tan; liver (red)-and-tan; and solid red. Small areas of white are permitted on the tail-tip, chest and feet.

Known throughout the world for its remarkable ability to follow scents and trails, the Bloodhound is a robust, powerful animal with a deep, gruff bark. It is also generally affectionate, good-natured and tolerant, but also somewhat reserved – even sensitive. Being so large, Bloodhounds must be handled correctly to avoid wilfulness and bad habits.

In films and stories, the Bloodhound is always depicted as a kind of sleuth or detective, which is due to its supposed ability to follow blood trails. However, the name actually refers to its aristocratic bloodline.

BORZOI

An ancient Russian breed, packs of Borzoi were once kept by almost all Russian noblemen. The largest Borzoi were used, in pairs, for bringing down wolves – as their original name 'Russian Wolfhound' suggests. The first Borzoi seen in England were presented to Queen Alexandra by the Russian tsar.

A graceful, aristocratic dog whose body suggests great power and speed, the long, lean head has a slightly domed skull. The jaws are long and powerful, and the nose is large and black. Eyes are dark, with an intelligent expression. The ears are small and pointed. The neck is slightly

arched and muscular. A Borzoi's body should be comparatively short, rising to an arch at the loins, and with a deep chest. The long, narrow legs are strong and muscular. The long tail is well-feathered.

The Borzoi has a silky, flat, curly or wavy coat, much longer on the body, and with feathering on the legs, chest, hindquarters and tail. Any colour is acceptable.

Rather aloof and self-possessed, this is by no means a typical pet dog, and some examples may be rather temperamental. Ownership should therefore be considered carefully. While the Borzoi may express affection for its owner, it is distrustful of strangers. For such a large animal, however, its appetite is not particularly large.

The Borzoi, the very personification of elegance, is not the ideal pet for everyone, being quiet and reserved and with a distrust of strangers and children.

COONHOUND

In the 17th century, British colonists imported Bloodhounds into the state of Virginia in America to be used as guards for the settlements. During the second half of the 18th century, with the aid of progeny from these early Bloodhounds, dogs were bred with the intention of hunting opossums and raccoons – especially at night. These dogs were given the name of Coonhounds, and of the various types developed, the most important is the Black-and-Tan.

The Coonhound is a large, powerful and alert dog with obvious Bloodhound ancestry. The head has a long, moderately-broad skull and a long, broad muzzle. The eyes are dark brown or hazel. The ears are long, pendulous and folded. The fairly long neck is carried on a medium-length body with a deep chest. Long, well-boned legs terminate in short, powerful feet. The tail is long and held erect when on the move.

There are several types of Coonhound: the Black-and-Tan, Bluetick, and English Coonhounds, the Plott Hound, and the Redbone and Treeing Walker Coonhounds.

A Black-and-Tan Coonhound (below left), a trail and tree hound, capable of withstanding the rigors of winter, the heat of summer, and the difficult terrain over which it is called upon to work, and a Redbone Coonhound (below), bred specifically to hunt raccoon.

As pets, Coonhounds are friendly by nature but can be aggressive when required, making good watchdogs with their impressive, loud barks.

DACHSHUND

The word Dachshund means 'badger dog' and describes the purpose for which these tough little dogs were originally bred in their native Germany. Their short legs and powerful jaws are ideal adaptations for entering setts and taking on their quarry underground. In fact, only the larger varieties were used for hunting badgers; the smaller ones hunted stoats and weasels. Not only did Dachshunds vary in size, however, but different coat-types was also developed, each coat-type being available in each size. Today, Dachshunds are popular show dogs as well as working dogs.

The Dachshund is a long and low dog with a muscular body. The long, lean head has a narrow skull and a long, fine muzzle. The eyes are medium-sized, almond-shaped and

Because Dachshunds are so near to the ground, care must be taken not to step upon them inadvertently. They are also prone to weight gain, so diet must be carefully monitored.

coloured dark reddish-brown to brown-black. The ears are broad, well-rounded and hang flat. The neck is rather long and muscular. A long body with a deep chest and level back must be held sufficiently clear of the ground to allow free movement. Legs are short and strong. The tail is long.

Dachshunds come in three coat-types: *Smoothhaired:* Short, glossy and dense. *Longhaired:* Soft and straight or slightly waved; abundant feathering on underside and behind legs. *Wirehaired:* Whole body, except for the chin, ears, jaws and eyebrows should be covered with short, straight, harsh hair. All colours are permissible.

Intelligent and lively, Dachshunds need firm training to control disobedience. Despite their small size, they make admirable watchdogs and are fearless in the protection of their family and friends, to whom they are very loyal. The Dachshund will normally eat whatever is placed before it – or whatever it may secure by its own means – so its diet should be firmly controlled.

DEERHOUND

One of the oldest of all the British breeds, the impressive-looking Deerhound was developed in the Scottish Highlands, having perhaps been brought originally to the country by Phoenician traders. Formally used to bring deer to bay, the ending of the clan system in Scotland following the Battle of Culloden in 1746 also meant the virtual demise of this noble breed. However, a few enthusiasts ensured its survival, and the dog still commands admiration and respect wherever it is seen.

The overall impression of a Deerhound is of a larger, bigger-boned, rough-coated Greyhound. The head is long with a broad skull, pointed muzzle and no stop. The nose should be black. The dark eyes appear gentle at rest but

BELOW, PAGES 148 & 149: The Deerhound resembles a large, hairy Greyhound. It is a noble breed with ancient origins which continues to be admired and respected to this day.

keen when aroused. The ears are small and folded back when the dog is at rest. A long, muscular neck is carried on a long body with well-arched loins and a deep chest. The legs are long and strongly boned. The tail is long and tapering, almost reaching the ground.

The coat is shaggy and thick; hard or crisp to the touch. The preferred colour is dark blue-grey, but darker or lighter greys, brindles and yellows, sandy-red or red-fawn also appear.

Speed, power and endurance are all suggested by the breed's build, but this is allied with a calm and dignified demeanour. The Deerhound is a gentle and friendly animal, ready to play and eager to please; considering its large size, it is remarkably easy to accommodate about the house.

ELKHOUND

An ancient Norwegian dog of the spitz type, which was used for hunting game, particularly elk. The Elkhound was developed for working in intensely cold conditions over rough terrain, and it is therefore no surprise that it should be so strong and hardy.

The Elkhound's head has a broad skull with a long, broad muzzle; there is a marked stop. The slightly oval eyes should have a fearless yet friendly, expression. The ears are erect and pricked. The powerful neck holds the head high. The short body has a deep chest with well-sprung ribs. Moderately long, strongly boned legs terminate in comparatively small, oval feet. The tail is held curled tightly over the back.

The dog has a coarse, straight, waterproof outercoat and a dense, soft, woolly undercoat. Colour can be

various shades of grey with black tips to the outercoat; lighter on the chest, stomach, legs and underside of the tail.

Hardy, bold and intelligent, the Elkhound is also friendly and independent with no sign of nervousness in its makeup. It has a loud and distinctive bark, and a fairly hearty appetite is a feature of this breed.

The Elkhound is a friendly, confident dog, with a dense waterproof coat that insulates it from the cold. It is hardy, has a very good appetite, and suffers from few genetic problems.

FINNISH SPITZ

The national dog of Finland, with a breed standard going back to at least 1812, the Finnish Spitz is one of several spitz breeds. Originally the dog was bred to track game, such as bear and elk, in Finnish woodlands and then to keep it at bay and mark its position with a piercing bark. Nowadays it is mainly used to track birds such as black grouse. The breed was introduced to Britain in 1927, and the first known import arrived in the United States in 1959. Puppies bear a strong resemblance to fox cubs.

The head of the Finnish Spitz is fox-like, with a gradually tapering muzzle. The medium to large eyes should be dark and have a lively expression, and the nose completely black. The pricked ears are small and sharply pointed. A muscular, medium-length neck is carried on a deep, almost square, body, the strong legs terminating in round feet. The bushy tail is held curled, typically spitz-like, over the back.

The coat is fairly long, with a short, dense undercoat which is shorter on the head and legs. Colour is a reddish-brown or red-gold on the back, with lighter shades in other parts.

Eager, courageous and intelligent, the Finnish Spitz is also lively and friendly. A good family pet but one that likes plenty of exercise, it is a rather vocal dog but with an undemanding appetite.

The foxy Finnish Spitz is lively and intelligent and makes a good pet, even though it was once used to track bear and elk in remote forests.

The Foxhound was bred specifically for hunting and is not usually regarded as a potential household pet. Given the correct training, however, this is not impossible, but the dog does require a good deal of exercise, having been developed to work hard all day long.

This is a dog with plenty of endurance and stamina, and with a natural hunting ability. The breed is also friendly and non-aggressive, although somewhat determined and ill-disciplined. With training, the Foxhound can be kept as a house dog, but it needs considerable exercise as well as feeding.

FOXHOUND

The Foxhound is a handsome dog whose purpose is exclusively to hunt – usually as part of a pack. As a result, the breed is seldom seen in the show ring and is not generally regarded as a potential household pet. Intense selection and careful breeding, free from the influences of fashion, have kept the Foxhound at the peak of perfection.

A well-balanced dog with a rather broad, medium-length skull and a fairly long muzzle. The medium-sized hazel or brown eyes should have a keen expression. The broad, moderately-long ears hang down flat. The neck is long and lean, and the body short and deep-chested. Long, well-boned legs terminate in round feet. The tail is long and is held aloft.

The Foxhound's coat is short, dense and waterproof. Any recognized hound colour is permissible, and includes combinations of black, tan and white.

combination of lemon, orange, tricolour or grizzled markings.

The Grand Basset Griffon Vendéen is a strong and active dog, possessing all the stamina required for a day's hunting. It is also an undemanding and outgoing breed, which enjoys the company of its owner. Regular grooming is required to keep the coat in good condition.

GRAND BASSET GRIFFON VENDÉEN

The origins of this breed can be traced back to the Vendée region of south-west France, where it was used for coursing hares and rabbits. The Grand Basset Griffon Vendéen was first introduced to Britain in 1990.

A well-balanced hound, it has a long skull, which is not too broad, with a long, square muzzle and slight stop. The nose should be large and black, the eyes large and dark, with an intelligent, friendly expression. The ears are long, thin and pendulous. A long body is carried on large, strong legs. The tail is fairly long and is proudly held.

The coat is rough and long, and of a flat nature with a thick undercoat. The colour can be white with any

This is a strong and active dog, once used for hare coursing in its native Vendée, where it was bred for stamina and the ability to keep going all day long.

GRAND BLEU DE GASCOIGNE

A descendant of the Grands Chiens Courants, it is said that King Henry IV of France owned a pack of these dogs. The Grand Bleu de Gascoigne is a hunter, like all hounds, originally hunting wolves, but going for hares today. The breed has only fairly recently been introduced as a show dog.

This is an aristocratic-looking dog with distinctive blue-tinged coloration. It has a large, long skull and muzzle.

The dark, chestnut-coloured eyes have a sad, gentle but trusting expression. The ears are thin, long and pendulous. The neck is characteristically throaty. The long, deep-chested body is carried on long, strongly boned legs. The tail is long and rather thick.

The coat is smooth and weather-resistant. There are speckles of black and larger black patches on white, producing the characteristic blueish tinge. Black patches also encircle the eyes and ears, and there is often a small

black patch on the skull. There are tan markings above the eyes, on the cheeks, lips, inside the ears, on the legs, and under the tail.

A dog with a powerful voice but a gentle disposition, the breed is sometimes described as lacking in energy. Although not suitable for all owners, the Grand Bleu is nevertheless affectionate and friendly.

A pack of the Grand Bleu de Gascoigne was said to have been owned by Henry IV of France, when they were used to hunt wolves. Today they lead less exciting lives and have recently been introduced to the show ring.

GREYHOUND

Many experts believe the Greyhound has its origins in the Middle East, in that drawings of dogs resembling the breed were found on the walls of ancient Egyptian tombs dating back to 4000 BC. The first of the so-called sighthounds, or gazehounds, the breed was eventually developed to today's standard in Britain, the racing Greyhound being slightly smaller than the show dog. Racing Greyhounds have been credited with attaining speeds of over 45mph (72kph), making them one of the fastest of all animals.

A large, strongly-built, muscular and symmetrical animal, the head is long with a broad skull and a long, strong muzzle. The dark eyes give an impression of intelligence. The ears are small and rose-shaped. The neck is long and muscular, and a deep and capacious chest allows for plenty of heart room. The back is long with powerful muscles, and there are slightly arched loins. Long, strongly boned legs terminate in long feet. The tail is long.

The Greyhound has a fine coat which lies close to the body. Colours may be black, white, red, fawn, brindle

Greyhounds have a natural inclination to chase smaller animals, which is why they will follow a mechanical prey around a track so readily.

or fallow, or any combination of these colours with white.

Greyhounds possess remarkable endurance and stamina and, of course, a turn of speed second to none in the canine world, facilitated by the animal's long-reaching stride over the ground. Quiet, calm and affectionate, but with a natural desire to chase other, smaller animals, they nevertheless make good pets and companions.

HAMILTONSTOVARE

One of the most popular breeds in its native Sweden, the Hamiltonstovare was created by Count Hamilton, the founder of the Swedish Kennel Club, in the 1800s. Also known as the Swedish Foxhound, the breed is used for hunting, but singly rather than as part of a pack.

The breed's Foxhound ancestry is clearly visible in this handsome and well-proportioned dog. The head is longish and rectangular, with a moderately-broad skull. The nose should always be black, the dark-brown eyes conveying a feeling of calm. The soft ears are approximately half the muzzle length, and the long, powerful neck merges into the shoulders. The back is straight and powerful and the chest is deep. The strong legs should appear parallel when viewed from front and back. The long tail is held straight or slightly curving up.

The outercoat is waterproof and lies close to the body, the undercoat being short and soft. The back is black, shading to brown on head and legs. There is white on the muzzle, neck, chest, lower legs and tail-tip.

An active dog which expects to work and exercise, this even-tempered hound also makes an undemanding companion. Happiest out in the countryside chasing a trail, the Hamiltonstovare will also adapt well to town life when the need arises.

The Hamiltonstovare is an adaptable dog and although it will tolerate life in town, its ancestry dictates it is more at home in the country.

IBIZAN HOUND

In the tomb of the pharaoh Hemako was found a carved dish bearing an image of an Ibizan Hound. The dish was made in the 1st Dynasty, between 3100 and 2700 BC, thus indicating that the history of the breed can be traced at least back to the time of the ancient Egyptians; the tombs of other such Egyptians also bear witness to the fact. Taking its name from the Balearic island of Ibiza, it was probably taken

there by Phoenician traders, having been known on the island, and on nearby Formentera, for at least 5,000 years. The Ibizan Hound is used for hunting hare, partridge and other game, either singly or as part of a pack.

A finely-built dog with upright ears, the head has a long, narrow skull and muzzle. The nose is flesh-coloured, the eyes are amber-coloured and fairly small. The ears are large and pricked. A long, lean neck is carried on a body with a long, flat ribcage and arched loins. The legs are long and strong and terminate in hare-like feet. The tail is long and thin.

The coat may be smooth or rough but is always dense and hard; it is longer under the tail. The colour can be white, 'lion' colour; or any combination of these colours.

Renowned jumpers, the breed needs plenty of space in which to exercise. Sometimes aloof with strangers, it is nevertheless devoted to its owner, being also intelligent, cheerful and non-aggressive.

This is one of the most ancient of breeds, depicted in artefacts from thousands of years ago. It is still going strong, being as intelligent and non-aggressive as ever.

IRISH WOLFHOUND

No other dog elicits such looks of admiration as the Irish Wolfhound. This magnificent breed was known to the ancient Romans, and it was held in great esteem from the 12th to the 16th century in Ireland, where it was used to hunt wolf, bear, stag and elk. When the last wolf was wiped out in Ireland, the Irish Wolfhound almost became extinct as well. In the mid 19th century, however, the breed was revived using the few remaining specimens. Now a healthy and enthusiastic following exists for these animals – the tallest of any of the breeds of dog.

Wolfhounds are of commanding size and appearance, coupled with

The Irish Wolfhound is an ancient breed, admired since Roman times for its huge size and dignified appearance. But it is a gentle giant, being even-tempered and good with children.

muscular strength. The head is long, and the skull not too broad. The muzzle is long and moderately pointed.

DOGS

The nose is black. The eyes are dark. The small rose-shaped ears have a fine, velvety texture. The neck is long and muscular. A long body with a very deep chest and arched loins is carried on long, well-boned legs. The tail is long and held slightly curved.

The coat is rough, hard and shaggy, being long and wiry over the eyes and under the jaw. Colours are black, grey, red, brindle, fawn, wheaten, steel-grey or pure white.

The breed's comparative rarity and huge size, together with its dignified air, set it apart from others. Despite being such a large dog, the breed is renowned for its calm and friendly nature. It is also tolerant of children and obedient. As befits such a massive creature, food portions need to be considerable to satisfy its appetite.

NORWEGIAN LUNDEHUND

This smallish dog originated on islands off the coast of Norway, and it is still relatively rare outside its native land, where it was used to search out puffins and their eggs along the coast – hence the word *lunde*, meaning puffin in Norwegian. The dog is unusual in that it has six toes on each foot – a selective adaptation that helped it in its task of climbing rocks.

The Norwegian Lundehund is a spitz-type dog of fairly light build. The wedge-shaped head has a fairly broad skull and a medium-length muzzle. The eyes are brown, and the mobile ears are pricked and of medium size. The strong neck is carried on a rectangular body with a strong, straight back. The legs are strong and carry double dew claws. The tail is sometimes carried curled up.

The dog has a dense, rough outercoat and a softer undercoat. Colours are shades of black, red-brown or grey, with white.

This is a good-natured, lively dog which is both alert and intelligent.

The Lundehund is unusual in that it has six toes on each foot, a selective adaptation that in a previous incarnation helped it to climb rocks.

chested body. Moderately long legs terminate in large, round feet which are webbed. The tail is thick at the base and tapers to a point.

The dog has a dense, harsh and waterproof double coat, the fur on the head and lower legs being softer. A slight oily texture may be apparent in the coat. All recognized hound colours are permitted.

The Otterhound was developed to spend much time hunting in the water, but the breed can also travel long

The affable Otterhound isn't the most elegant of creatures, but it has great stamina and its engaging personality makes it a rewarding pet.

distances across rough country without tiring. A loud, baying bark and a keen nose for a scent are other features of this dog, and it is also good-natured, intelligent and friendly. Not the most stylish-looking dog by any means, the Otterhound makes up for this by having an engaging personality.

OTTERHOUND

With an ancestry that includes French blood mixed with various strains of English hounds, the Otterhound is a long-established breed; a pack of Otterhounds was known to have been kept by the English King John in 1212. When in 1977 the hunting of otters was banned in England and Wales, the breed declined. A campaign to have the breed recognized in Britain for showing purposes helped to restore its fortunes.

A large, rugged-looking dog, the head is heavy with a medium to broad skull and a deep muzzle. The entire head is covered with rough fur. The eyes are brown, helping to convey an amiable expression. The ears are long and pendulous. A long and powerful neck is carried on a strong, deep-

PETIT BASSET GRIFFON VENDÉEN

A breed originating in France, the word *basset* indicates a dog that is low to the ground, and it is used by sportsmen for trailing and beating game from cover. Introduced into Britain in 1969, this is still a comparatively rare breed.

A compact, short-legged hound, the head, carried on a long, strong neck, has a medium-length skull. The nose is black, and the large, dark eyes convey intelligence and friendliness. The supple ears end in oval shapes and are covered with long, fine hair. The medium-length body has a deep chest and is carried on thick, well-boned legs. The tail is of medium length and carried proudly.

The dog has a rough, long outercoat with a thick undercoat. Colour is white with any combination of orange, lemon, tricolour or grizzle.

Like most hounds, this dog is happiest out in the countryside following trails. The dog's expression exemplifies its character – extrovert, happy and alert.

This is a country dog at heart and likes nothing better than to sniff around, searching out a trail. This amiable little dog would make an ideal companion for a country-dweller.

PHARAOH HOUND

This is the national dog of Malta, where it is called the Kelb tal-Fenek, meaning 'rabbit hound'. It is indigenous to the island and remains rare outside of Malta. It is number 141 out of 154 breeds registered in 2005 by the American Kennel Club. It was once thought to be the dog depicted on pottery and other artefacts found in the tombs of the ancient Egyptians, which has since been disproved. But the myth persists.

Graceful, and with a noble bearing, the head has a long skull and a long muzzle with a slight stop. The small, amber-coloured eyes are oval and intelligent. The ears are pricked. A long, lean and strong neck is carried on a long body with a deep chest. The legs are long and well-boned. The long tail is held high and curved when on the move.

The coat is fine or slightly harsh; short and glossy. The colour is a rich tan but with a white tail-tip, a white mark on the chest and white toes. A slim white blaze on the centre of the face is also acceptable.

An alert hunter that tracks its prey by both scent and sight, this is a true working hound; at the same time it is also friendly and affectionate, and willing to play. The short coat means the dog should not be exposed to very cold conditions without protection.

The Pharaoh Hound has a noble bearing, being an excellent hunter that tracks its prey by scent as well as sound. Coming fom the Mediterranean, and having a short coat, it needs added protection in cold climates.

RHODESIAN RIDGEBACK

The Rhodesian Ridgeback was developed by crossing dogs, brought to southern Africa by European farmers, with native hunting dogs. This produced a large breed of dog that was ideal for hunting game and also for guarding. The original native dogs had a ridge on their back, and this feature is a characteristic of the Rhodesian Ridgeback. The dog was introduced to Rhodesia (now Zimbabwe) in the 1870s and was bred there in large numbers – which is the reason it was given the name of that country.

The head has a broad skull with a long, deep muzzle. The nose is black or

brown. The eyes are round and bright and should tone in with the coat-colour. The medium-sized ears are pendulous. The muscular body is fairly long and supports a long, strong neck. The legs are strong and muscular. The tail is carried with a slight upward curve but never curled.

The Rhodesian Ridgeback has a short and dense coat, with a glossy, sleek appearance; the ridge of hair on the back should be clearly defined, tapering and symmetrical. Colour is light wheaten to red wheaten, with only small amounts of white on the chest and toes.

Powerful and agile, the Rhodesian Ridgeback is a loyal and protective dog towards its family. It is not necessarily the ideal choice for the inexperienced, however.

The Rhodesian Ridgeback is a large, muscular dog requiring correct training. It is loyal and protective, but is not the first choice for the inexperienced handler.

SALUKI

One of the oldest of the North African breeds of dog, the Saluki is depicted on the carvings of tombs in Sumeria and Egypt dating from 7000 BC. A breed much prized by Arabs, the dog has a keen hunting instinct and is renowned for the speed with which it moves over the variable Middle Eastern terrain. Despite its ancient lineage, the Saluki was not seen in Europe until the 1840s. Its name may come from either the former Arabian city of Saluk or from Seleukia in ancient Syria.

THIS PAGE & PAGES 166 & 167: The Saluki is the oldest of the African breeds and has been depicted in ancient artefacts. Loyal to its owner, it is highly-strung and becomes easily bored if left to its own devices.

The overall impression of the Saluki is of grace and speed. The long, narrow head tapers towards the nose, which is black or liver. The muzzle is long and strong. The large eyes are dark to light brown in colour, with an intelligent, interested expression. The long, mobile ears are covered with long, silky fur. The body, like the neck, is long. The chest is deep with slightly arched ribs. Long, powerful legs and feet and a long, well-feathered tail complement the other features.

The coat is soft and silky, longer on the ears, with feathering on the legs, back of thighs and tail. Colours are white, cream, fawn, red, grizzle, silver grizzle, tricolour (black, white and tan), black-and-tan, and permutations of these colours.

A speedy and active hunter, with a far-seeing gaze, the breed is dignified and gentle, but can become bored and destructive if left alone. Although somewhat reserved with strangers, and even highly-strung, the dog is very affectionate towards its owner.

SEGUGIO ITALIANO

Also known as the Italian Hound, this is an ancient breed, thought to be descended from Celtic hounds. Traditionally, the Segugio Italiano was used to hunt wild boar in its native Italy, but the end of the great hunts saw the numbers of pure-bred dogs decline. Interest in the breed was revived in the 20th century, and numbers were increased by careful breeding, so that today the dog is extremely popular in Italy both for hunting a variety of game and as a companion, although it remains rare and relatively unknown outside its native land.

A medium-sized hound of light build with a squarish outline, the head is fine, long and with a narrow skull and muzzle. The nose is black, and the eyes are large, dark and oval. The fine, triangular ears can reach to the tip of the nose. A long, lean neck is carried on a moderately long body with a deep chest. The legs are long and strong. The tail is thin and tapering and is carried upwardly curved when on the move.

The short coat can be either smooth or harsh, and in both types the hairs are close-lying. Colours are black-and-tan or any tone from deep-red to wheaten. White marks on the head, chest, feet and tail-tip are permitted.

A versatile and active hunter with great stamina, this is nevertheless a fairly quiet breed that is both gentle and affectionate, although some individuals have been known to resent strangers.

The Segugio Italiano is an ancient breed that, although quiet and affectionate, also has great stamina. It is uncertain with strangers, and a firm hand is required.

SLOUGHI

This elegant and lean-looking breed has existed in the desert and mountainous regions of North Africa for centuries, where it is utilized as a sighthound. It is likely that the dog was a native of the Middle East before it was brought to Africa. This is neither a common dog on the European scene, nor one that has ever achieved wide popularity.

The overall impression is of a racy but delicate dog. The head is strong, but not heavy, and the skull is flat and fairly broad. There is a wedge-shaped muzzle. The nose is black or dark brown. The large eyes are set well into their orbits, the expression being gentle, if a little sad. The ears are triangular and pendulous. The strong and elegant neck is carried on a deep-chested body with prominent haunches. Legs are long and well-muscled. The long tail is never carried higher than the back when the dog is on the move.

The coat is smooth and fine, the most usual colours being shades of fawn or sable, while brindle, white or black with tan points can also occur; a black mask may also be present. The accepted standard is for prominent haunches, and this may deter some because of the fine line that exists between this requirement and unattractive thinness.

The Sloughi is a calm, clean and graceful-looking dog, much valued as a hunter and a guard. Aloof with strangers, it is nevertheless affectionate towards its owner.

The Sloughi is an elegant North African hound, slightly wary of strangers, but always loyal and affectionate towards its owner.

WHIPPET

Despite appearances, the Whippet is not a small Greyhound. It came about in the 19th century when it became legal in Britain for working people to hunt small game and vermin. Originally called a 'snap-dog', the term may have been coined either because of the animal's ability to snap up small game, such as rabbits, or because of the English word 'snap', meaning food – a reference to the dog's ability to provide food for its owner. The Whippet's speed also made it a popular subject for racing, and races often took place in the alleyways between houses when no other venues were available.

Whippets are muscular and powerful but at the same time graceful and elegant. The head is long and lean with a tapering muzzle. The nose should be black or of a colour toning with the body colour. The oval eyes are bright and lively. The ears are fine and rose-shaped. A long, well-muscled neck is supported by a fairly long body with a

deep chest and arched loins; the loins should give an impression of power and muscularity. The legs are long and strong. The tail is long and tapering.

The Whippet's coat is fine, dense and short. Any colour or mixture of colours is permitted.

A highly adaptable sporting dog that is happy out in the field, at home with the family, or trotting at heel when out on a walk. A deservedly popular pet, it is both gentle and affectionate. The Whippet is also neat and tidy, easy to care for, and has an undemanding appetite.

The Whippet may appear to be too slight and delicate to be capable of much, but don't be fooled: this is a highly valued sporting dog, with a legendary turn of speed.

Chapter Four
UTILITY DOGS

The utility, or non-sporting, group includes dogs of many different shapes and sizes, and which perform a variety of tasks. The group ranges from the large breeds, such as the Japanese Akita and the Leonberger, to much smaller orientals like the Shih Tzu. The group is sometimes said to include the breeds that do not satisfactorily fit into any of the other main groups, such as gun dogs and terriers. A more useful classificatory criterion, however, might be to say that within the utility group are to be found dogs that are appreciated first and foremost for their companionship, but which may also undertake other useful roles such as guarding property. (This is not to say, however, that dogs from some of the other groups are not efficient guards or do not make good companions.)

But the breeds found within the utility group do seem to have an hereditary aptitude for defending and guarding. Some, like the Bulldog and the Japanese Akita, were originally bred as fighting dogs, and these aggressive

tendencies came into their own when required to stand guard. Even among the breeds which did not display these gladiatorial skills, there was a

propensity to give voice in no uncertain manner at the arrival of strangers to the door, making such animals ideal watchdogs. This is a virtue no less important today than it was in the past, for it is a well-known fact that a property guarded by a loudly barking dog is a much less attractive proposition for a would-be burglar than one which meets their arrival with silence. Although modern-day utility dogs are not especially pugnacious by nature, most will be prepared to respond appropriately if there is a real threat to the family or home which they think they have a responsibility for guarding.

Among the diverse shapes and sizes to be found within the utility group, one group of dogs stands out: the spitz breeds. Fairly uniform in type and appearance, spitzes are of Arctic origin, and these hardy animals were bred to work in the harsh and inhospitable conditions of the frozen north. They all have compact, muscular bodies and loud voices. Among the adaptations designed to help reduce heat loss from the body are thick, insulating coats, hooded ears, and tails that are usually held curled over the back, close to the body. Spitz dogs were, and in some places still are, expected to perform a wide range of tasks. These include guarding domestic animal herds, working as watchdogs, hunting, and acting as draft dogs, i.e. pulling sleds or carrying tents and other equipment on their backs. They probably served another useful function by being something warm to curl up against at night.

Another group of utility dogs, the schnauzers, are sometimes called German terriers. They do not bark with the frequency that characterizes spitz dogs, but they are generally considered to be more intelligent. The larger versions of schnauzers, in particular, can be rather wilful unless correctly trained to bring out their best qualities. They also need to be handled properly to prevent them from trying to get the upper hand.

Some of the other dogs within the utility group can also be trained to perform useful tasks over and above those of guard or companion. The Dalmatian, being a keen and powerful runner, can be trained for hunting and retrieving, while Poodles, too, have considerable retrieving skills, being particularly adept at gathering from water. Poodles, among other animals, are also sometimes used to sniff out truffles lying hidden below ground.

OPPOSITE: The Leonberger never seems to be in a hurry, being happy to amble along at its own speed. An easy-going, friendly dog, it can nevertheless give a good account of itself as a guard dog.

LEFT: Poodles are intelligent creatures, once highly prized as performing animals in circuses and stage shows due to their ability quickly to learn new tricks.

BOSTON TERRIER

The ancestors of this American breed include Bulldogs and Bull Terriers. Derived from pit fighting dogs, the first of the breed appeared in the 1890s around Boston. The animal is striking in appearance, and is often regarded as the national dog of America, where, and to a lesser extent in Britain, it is a popular show dog and companion.

A muscular dog with distinctive, erect ears and a striking coat, the head is square with a short, wide muzzle. The nose is black, and the large, round eyes are set widely apart, producing an alert expression. The slightly arched neck is carried on a short, deep-chested body. The legs are strong and muscular. The tail is short and tapering, and may be straight or screw.

The coat is short and glossy. Brindle-and-white are the preferred colours, but black-and-white is also permissible.

The Boston Terrier is a dapper-looking, small to medium-sized dog. It is strong-willed and determined, but nevertheless makes an amiable and intelligent housedog.

America's iconic breed, the Boston Terrier is an attractive little dog. It can be strong-willed and will benefit from training, but its useful size and cheerful disposition makes it an admirable companion.

BULLDOG

One of the most instantly recognizable breeds, the Bulldog is the national dog of Britain and is known the world over as a symbol of indomitable spirit and determination. The history of the Bulldog probably stretches back to at least the 1600s, when it was used in bull-baiting and dog fights. Fortunately this, and similar barbaric pursuits, were abolished in the 19th century, and the dog became a show dog and companion instead, the ferocity of earlier individuals having been bred out.

A massively-built, low and sturdy dog, the head is also massive and deep, with a broad, square skull and a short, broad muzzle with an upturned lower jaw. The nose is black. The eyes are round, set widely apart, and have a quizzical and appealing expression. The rose ears are small. The neck is very thick, deep and powerful. The body is short, broad in front and narrow towards the rear; the chest is deep and broad. The fore legs are stout and placed far apart so that they can appear slightly bowed, although the bones themselves are actually straight; the hind legs are longer. The tail is rather short and tapers to a fine point.

The coat is fine, close and short. Colours are whole or smut (in other words, a whole colour with a black

muzzle or mask), brindles, reds plus shades such as fawn, white and pied (in other words, white with any of the aforementioned colours).

The Bulldog's pugilistic appearance belies an affectionate nature. Somewhat stubborn and tenacious on occasions, the breed is nevertheless good with children and makes a protective watchdog when required. It can also be humorous – even comical – which adds to its charm. Would-be owners should note that, although the Bulldog can show a good turn of speed when needed, it usually prefers to proceed at a more leisurely pace.

Synonymous with quiet determination, the English Bulldog is described as having an indomitable spirit.

CANAAN DOG

This is the national dog of Israel. It was selectively bred from pariah dogs, the feral or semi-wild dogs that are common in parts of North Africa and countries of the Middle East. This is a comparatively rare breed outside its native land.

The Canaan is a medium-sized, well-balanced dog. The wedge-shaped head has a fairly flat skull and a moderate to broad muzzle. The nose is black, and the almond-shaped eyes are dark. The prominent ears are erect and broad at the base. The body is square, with a level back and muscular loins. The legs are long and strong and end in round, cat-like feet. The tail is long and bushy, and is held curled over the back when on the move.

The coat is straight, hard and of medium length. Colours are sandy to tan, black, white or spotted; white markings are permissible in all colours.

Alert and intelligent, the Canaan Dog can be rather aloof with strangers but makes a good watchdog.

The Canaan is an attractive, medium-sized dog, rare outside the Middle East. It tends to be wary of strangers, making it an effective guard dog.

CHOW CHOW

A spitz-type dog that has been known in China for about 2,000 years, but because China was closed to outsiders for long periods in its history, the breed did not appear in other countries until the 1800s. In China, the dog was used as a guard, a companion, and for hunting – it was even used as a source of food! There are two types of the Chow Chow: the smooth-coated and the rough-coated.

A heavy-looking, woolly-coated dog with a lion-like appearance, the head has a heavy, broad skull and a medium-length, broad muzzle. The nose is black. The gums, roof of the mouth and tongue are blue-black. The eyes are dark and oval-shaped. The ears are small and pricked. A strong neck is carried on a short, broad, deep-chested body. The legs are heavily-boned and muscular. The tail is carried curled over the back.

The outercoat is coarse, thick and abundant in the rough-coated dog, being especially profuse around the neck and behind the legs; the undercoat

is soft and woolly. In smooth-coated dogs the coat is short, dense, straight and plush. Colours are solid black, red, blue, cream, fawn or white.

In general, the Chow Chow does not take readily to strangers, despite being loyal towards its owner. Rather independent, and seldom moving at great speed, this is a quiet dog that may not appeal to everyone.

Quiet and sedate, the Chow Chow is not everyone's idea of the perfect pet. It is unsuited to hot climates due to the thickness of its coat.

DALMATIAN

Instantly recognizable by anyone with a passing interest in dogs, the Dalmatian was highly popular in Britain during the Regency period, when it was also known as a 'carriage dog', due to its habit of running alongside, or even beneath, all kinds of carriages. It also used to run in front of horse-drawn fire engines in both Britain and America. The ability to run in such a way was possible because of the great stamina and endurance possessed by the breed. Today, the Dalmatian is a popular, friendly and long-lived pet.

A clean-looking, elegant, and athletic dog with a distinctive coat pattern, the head is fairly long, with a broad skull and a long, strong muzzle. The nose is black in black-spotted varieties and brown in liver-spotted individuals. The eyes are dark or amber, according to the coat-colour; they should look bright and express intelligence. The ears are fairly large and pendulous. A long, well-arched neck is carried on a deep-chested body with a powerful back. The legs are long

Having abundant energy itself, the Dalmation makes a rewarding pet for a similarly active owner with the time and will to exercise and train it correctly.

and muscular. The tail is long and carried with a slight upward curve when on the move.

The coat is short, dense, glossy and sleek. The ground colour is pure white, evenly covered with either black or liver spots.

The Dalmatian has great freedom of movement, using a long-striding, rhythmic action to cover the ground. A good sporting dog if required – with boundless energy and enthusiasm – the breed is also the perfect housedog and companion for an active owner.

FRENCH BULLDOG

Working in France in the 1850s, lace-makers from England took their small Bulldogs with them, where it is thought they were bred with local French dogs, thus producing the French Bulldog. The French Bulldog was then introduced back to Britain in the early part of the 20th century.

A small, sturdy and compact dog with characteristic 'bat' ears, the head is square, with a broad, short skull and muzzle. The nose is black. The eyes are round and set forward in the head, producing a trusting expression. The bat ears are wide at the base and held upright and parallel. The powerful neck is carried on a short, muscular body with a deep chest. The legs are short and powerful, the hind legs being longer than the front legs. The tail is short and thick at the root.

The coat is short, close, glossy and smooth. Colours are brindle, pied or fawn.

Like the British Bulldog, breathing can be somewhat restricted in the French Bulldog, therefore it may be inclined to take things at its own pace from time to time – although it can rush about well enough when the need arises. This is a jolly, affectionate and endearing breed which is quiet in the house and only too happy to curl up with family and friends.

This sturdy little dog, like other bulldog types, can suffer restricted breathing and likes to take things at its own pace. When it has a mind, however, it can be active enough.

GERMAN SPITZ

In Germany, there are five different varieties of spitz dogs, ranging in size from the large Wolfspitz to the small Pomeranian. The two varieties described here are the *klein* (small) and the *mittel* (medium) varieties. Apart from the difference in size, they are identical.

A compact, full-coated dog with erect ears. The head has a broad, flattish skull with the muzzle narrowing to a wedge. The nose is either black or a colour harmonizing with the coat. The eyes are dark; either black or a tone harmonizing with the coat-colour. The small ears are held completely erect. The body is short,

with well-developed loins. The legs are well boned and terminate in cat-like feet. The tail is curled and held up over the back.

The double coat consists of a long, hard, straight outercoat and a soft, woolly undercoat. The fur is very thick around the neck and forequarters. All colours are acceptable, including chocolate, white and fawn.

Cheerful and friendly, and with an undemanding appetite, the German Spitz enjoys being part of a family. Its long coat will keep it warm in the coldest weather, but requires regular and thorough grooming.

The German Spitz makes a fine pet and has a cheerful personality, but will require careful grooming to safeguard its beautiful coat.

JAPANESE AKITA

Also known as the Akita Inu, meaning 'large dog', this is Japan's largest and best-known breed. Its origins can be traced to northern polar regions, the spitz-type dogs eventually reaching northern Japan. Similar dogs were depicted in reliefs dating back to 2000 BC, and the history of the Akita itself can be traced back 300 years. Originally used for fighting, as well as for hunting bears and wild boar, the breed is now used mainly as a guardian and army dog.

The Akita is an immensely powerful and striking dog with a bear-like face. The head has a fairly broad skull and a medium-length, strong muzzle. The nose is black. The small, almond-shaped eyes are brown. The hooded ears are fairly small, triangular, and set widely apart; they are held firmly erect. A thick, muscular neck is carried on a body with a deep, wide chest and a level back. The legs are well-boned, strong and muscular. The tail is large, and is carried curled over the back.

The double coat consists of a coarse, straight outercoat and a soft undercoat. The coat may be of any colour, such as white, brindle or grey,

but should be brilliant and clear; a contrasting mask is often present.

A dog of impressive appearance and with a character to match, this is not a typical family dog by any means. The Japanese Akita is reserved and protective but clearly likes to dominate; it requires firm control from its owner to remind it who is in charge.

The Japanese Akita, though brave and affectionate, has a will to dominate that must be kept firmly under control.

JAPANESE SHIBA INU

Shiba Inu means 'small dog', and the breed resembles a small Japanese Akita. The Shiba Inu comes from Japan's mountainous inland regions, where it is sometimes used to hunt game. The breed is popular in its native country and is slowly becoming more available elsewhere.

A sturdy spitz-type dog, the head appears triangular viewed from above; the skull is broad, and with a short muzzle. The nose is usually black but may be flesh-coloured in white-coated dogs. The small, almond-shaped eyes are brown. The hooded ears are fairly small, triangular, and inclined slightly forward; they are held firmly erect. A

thick, muscular neck is carried on a body with a deep, wide chest. The legs are moderately long and muscular and end in cat-like feet. The tail is large, carried curled over the back.

The double coat consists of a coarse, straight outercoat and a soft undercoat. Colours are red, black, black-and-tan, brindle, or white with a grey or red tinge.

The Shiba Inu is a much better choice of family pet than the larger but similar-looking Akita, being a good, but not over-noisy, watchdog with a lively and playful personality.

Similar to the Japanese Akita, the Shiba Inu is somewhat smaller and makes a more manageable pet. As a puppy it is very boisterous, but given the correct training it should eventually calm down.

JAPANESE SPITZ

This small breed stemmed originally from Nordic spitz stock, brought to Japan early in the 20th century, where it was bred on to reduce its size. From Japan, the dog was exported to Sweden and other countries.

A small, spitz-type dog with a profuse, bushy coat, the head has a moderate to broad skull and a pointed muzzle. The nose is black. The eyes are dark and oval-shaped. The small triangular ears are held slightly forward and erect. The neck is strong and is carried on a deep-chested body with a short, straight back. The legs terminate in cat-like feet. The tail is of moderate length and is held curled over the back.

The Japanese Spitz has an outercoat which is straight and stand-off, and there is a short, thick, soft undercoat. The coat-colour is pure white.

This is a nimble and active little dog with an attractive, friendly nature and good guarding instincts. The breed does not require excessive amounts of exercise or food, but the coat will need regular attention to keep it looking its best.

The Japanese Spitz makes a good family pet, being small, good-natured, and requiring only moderate amounts of food and exercise to keep it happy.

KEESHOND

The Keeshond takes its name from the Dutch patriot, Cornelius de Gyselaer, whose nickname was 'Kees'. The dog was adopted as a mascot in the years before the French Revolution, although it already had long associations as a watchdog for Dutch bargemen and is still known as the Dutch Bargedog. The dog's popularity declined somewhat in the years leading up to 1920, but was revived through the efforts of Baroness von Hardenbroek, who bred some fine examples. Today, the breed's excellent guarding instincts are still employed, and the dog is a popular family companion.

The Keeshond is a compact, spitz-type dog with a bushy coat. The fox-like head has a moderate to broad skull and a narrowing muzzle. The nose is black. The eyes are dark and almond-shaped. The small triangular ears are held erect. The neck is moderately long and arched, and is carried on a short and compact body. The legs are strongly muscled and terminate in cat-like feet. The tail is of moderate length and is held curled tightly over the back.

The dog's outercoat is harsh, straight and stand-off, and there is a short, thick, soft undercoat. The coat forms a dense ruff at the neck, as well as providing good feathering on the legs above the hocks. The coat-colour is a mixture of black and grey.

A delightful, trusting and cheerful dog, the Keeshond is patient with children and ready for anything. Alert to every sound, it makes an excellent watchdog, and it is happy to be out even in the coldest weather; its

The Keeshound, also known as the Dutch Bargedog, is an amiable breed and its alertness to every sound makes it an excellent watchdog.

luxuriant coat, however, means that grooming needs to be regular and thorough.

LEONBERGER

This very substantial dog, the result of crossing St Bernards with Newfoundlands, comes from Leonberg in Germany, where the mayor decided to create a new breed in honour of the town in 1840. An even-tempered and intelligent dog, the breed fell into serious decline between the First and Second World Wars, but in due course, the few remaining specimens were used to re-establish the breed.

The Leonberger is a large, purposeful-looking dog with a medium-length coat. The head has a fairly wide skull and a broad, square muzzle. The dark eyes have a friendly, intelligent expression. The pendulous ears are well-feathered and with rounded tips. The strong neck is carried on a deep-chested body. The legs are well-boned, strong and muscular, ending in webbed feet. The tail is long and carried 'at half mast'.

The coat is of medium length, varying in texture from fairly soft to hard; it may be wavy but never curly. Colours are yellow or golden to red-brown, preferably with a black mask.

The Leonberger never seems to be in a hurry, being happy to amble along at its own speed. An easy-going,

friendly dog, the Leonberger can nevertheless give a good account of itself when called upon to guard the household. The breed prefers the outdoor life and is a keen swimmer, as suggested by its webbed feet. Being such a large dog, the Leonberger has a very hearty appetite.

The Leonberger is an easy-going dog, but its huge size means that it is not the ideal pet for everyone. However, it makes a good guard dog and is an excellent swimmer.

LHASA APSO

This little dog originated in Tibet, where it was used mainly as a house watchdog. Many of these dogs live at high altitudes in the mountainous countryside, and the breed's long coat and warm undercoat, together with the generous covering of hair over the face, help keep them warm. Apsos first appeared in Britain in the 1920s, and they are also popular in other Western countries, including America.

A solid dog with a long coat, the head has a medium to narrow skull and a blunt muzzle. The nose is black, and the oval eyes are dark brown. The pendulous ears have a very generous covering of hair. A long neck is carried on a long, deep-chested body. The legs are short and terminate in cat-like feet. The tail is carried curled over the back.

The dog's outercoat is long, straight and hard; the undercoat is dense. Colours range from golden, sandy, honey, grizzle, slate, smoke, parti-colour, black, white and brown.

The Lhasa Apso is alert and watchful, and strangers to the house are liable to be greeted with frenzied barking – which explains the breed's popularity as a watchdog. But where its family and friends are concerned, the dog is affectionate and cheerful, and hardy enough to be taken for long walks. The coat needs regular careful grooming to prevent it from becoming hopelessly matted.

The Lhasa Apso is a hardy little dog, more than able to cope with long walks. Daily grooming is vital to keep its long and luxurious coat in good condition.

MINIATURE SCHNAUZER

This bright and lively German dog is believed to have been developed when a Schnauzer was crossed with an Affenpinscher. The Miniature Schnauzer has much of the terrier in its appearance and character – and indeed, in America, it is placed within the terrier group. Schnauzers come in two other sizes, Standard and Giant, in addition to the Miniature Schnauzer described here.

A sturdy, alert-looking dog of nearly square proportions, the head is long with a flat skull and strong

muzzle. The nose is black, and the dark eyes are oval and set forward in the skull. The V-shaped ears are usually folded forward, although in some countries they may be cropped. The arched, moderate to long neck is carried on a short body with a fairly deep chest. The legs are well-boned and muscular. The tail is usually docked.

The coat is rough and wiry, the face having a bushy beard and eyebrows. Colours are pure black, black-and-silver, or pepper-and-salt.

Alert and quick-moving, the Miniature Schnauzer makes the ideal companion – whether it be for an active family looking for a dog to join in the fun, or for an older person wanting a trusted and loyal friend.

The Miniature Schnauzer is one of the most adaptable members of the utility group, but with a definite look of the terrier about it, and in America it is categorized as such. The ears are sometimes cropped, which is an illegal practice in some parts of the world.

POODLE

The Poodle, one of the most popular of breeds, comes in three sizes: Toy, Miniature and Standard. It is also usually one of the most recognizable of breeds, due mainly to the fact that its fur is often clipped into very distinctive shapes. Despite the somewhat unlikely appearance of some show poodles, the breed was originally used as a truffle-hunter and as a retriever, being especially adept at gathering from water. Although considered to be a French dog, it is more likely that the breed actually originated in Germany and was later taken to France. In some countries the Toy Poodle is placed in the toy group.

The poodle is an elegant-looking, balanced dog with a distinctive coat. The head is long, with a moderate to broad skull and a strong muzzle. The almond-shaped eyes are black or dark brown, and express intelligence and verve. The ears are long and hang close to the face. The neck is strong and carries the head with dignity. The body is broad and deep-chested, with powerful loins. The legs are long and well-boned. The tail is usually docked and is carried at a slight angle away from the body.

The coat is dense and profuse with a harsh texture; the coat does not moult, and it is often clipped into patterns, such as the lion clip or the less fussy Dutch clip. All solid colours are permitted.

Poodles are intelligent dogs, once highly prized as performing animals in circuses and stage shows due to their ability to learn quickly. The two smaller breeds are the most suited to a life in town, whereas the Standard is a real country dog at heart. All Poodles, however, are friendly, high-spirited dogs that make good pets.

Considered by many to be the most intelligent of the breeds, it is said that once you own a Poodle you will never look at another dog again.

The Schnauzer is a sturdy, well-built dog, the name referring to its distinctive moustache. It has a tendency to be aggressive towards people it doesn't know.

SCHNAUZER

The Schnauzer, also known as the Standard Schnauzer in America, is the middle-sized of the three Schnauzers. A German breed with a long history behind it, the dog was originally used to catch vermin, herd livestock, pull carts, and guard property.

A robust, almost square dog with an alert manner, the head has a rather broad skull and a fairly long, strong muzzle. The nose is black. The eyes are oval and dark. The V-shaped ears usually drop forward but in some countries are cropped. The neck is strong and slightly arched and is carried on a short body with a moderately-deep chest. The legs are muscular and well-developed, ending in cat-like feet. The tail is usually docked.

The outercoat is wiry, harsh and short with a dense undercoat; moustache, whiskers and eyebrows are prominent. Colours are either pure black or pepper-and-salt.

An outgoing and lively dog with a trustworthy nature, the Schnauzer looks fiercer than it actually is, which stands it in good stead when called upon to guard property. Fond of children and ever ready to work or play, the Schnauzer makes an ideal house dog.

SHAR PEI

A Chinese breed, the Shar Pei was originally bred for use as a guard, hunter and herding dog. This is a most unusual-looking dog, with a suggestion of Mastiff in its ancestry. Early examples in the West were short in the leg and unfortunately tended to suffer from a condition known as entropion (inward rolling of the eyelid), but the breed has been improved greatly in recent years. Devotees of the breed will not hear a word said against it, while others will find its looks distinctly not to their liking.

A squarely-built dog with a characteristically wrinkled skin and frowning expression. The head is rather large and rectangular, and the muzzle is long, broad and padded. The nose is preferably black, but any colour harmonizing with the coat-colour is allowed. The eyes are almond-shaped and may be dark or light, depending on the coat-colour. The ears are small, triangular and folded. The neck is short and strong. The body is short and deep and slightly raised under the loins. The legs are muscular and strong. The tail tapers at the tip and

may be carried high and curved or curled over the back.

The coat is bristly, short and hard and standing off from the body. Colours are solid black, red, cream, or fawn.

This is a vigorous and active dog. Early exports were reported to have temperamental problems, but the breed has been improved over the last ten or fifteen years.

The distinctively different Shar Pei needs a lot of attention to guard it against skin problems. While its unusual looks are not to everyone's taste, it nevertheless has its enthusiastic fans.

SHIH TZU

The Shih Tzu came originally from Tibet, although it was developed in China, where it found favour in the royal courts of the imperial palaces. Records dating back to AD 624 show dogs very similar to the Shih Tzu being given as tributes to the Tang emperor. The name Shih Tzu translates as 'lion dog', and is believed to be a reference to the dog's brave character rather than to its appearance. The first examples of this breed to be seen in Britain arrived in 1931. In America, the breed is placed within the toy group.

The Shih Tzu is a long-coated little dog with a very proud carriage. The head is broad and round with a short, square muzzle. The nose is usually black but may be liver-coloured in liver or liver-marked dogs. The eyes are large, round and dark and have a friendly expression. The ears are large and pendulous. The body is long with a deep chest. The legs are short, muscular and well-boned. The well-plumed tail is carried curled over the back.

The coat is long, straight and dense, with a dense undercoat; a slight wave is permitted in the coat, but not a curl; the hair should form a good beard and whiskers, and hair growing upward over the nose bridge should create the familiar 'chrysanthemum' look. All colours are permitted.

An outgoing, enthusiastic little dog, the Shih Tzu is also intelligent and friendly and makes a good family addition. Moderate exercise is all that is required, but regular grooming is necessary to keep the coat healthy and tangle-free.

The Shih Tzu is a fun-loving little dog and despite its small size has a confident and dignified air. Regular grooming is a necessity, however, and ears must be examined regularly for signs of infection.

TIBETAN SPANIEL

Bred in the border valleys between Tibet and China, this was one of the first of the Tibetan breeds to reach Britain, arriving in about 1900. In its native lands, it was popular among members of the royal courts as well as in monasteries.

A neat and tidy little dog, the head is slightly small in proportion with the body, and has a slightly domed skull with a shortish muzzle.

The nose is usually black. The dark-brown, oval eyes are of medium size and set widely apart but forward-looking. The medium-sized ears are pendulous. The neck is short and strong, carried on a longish body with a good chest and a level back. The legs are moderately boned, the fore legs being slightly bowed; the legs terminate in hare-like feet. The well-plumed tail is carried curled over the back.

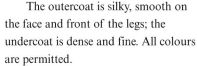

The outercoat is silky, smooth on the face and front of the legs; the undercoat is dense and fine. All colours are permitted.

Another of the small and dignified oriental breeds, the Tibetan Spaniel is nevertheless quite happy to have mad sessions racing around the garden. Somewhat aloof with strangers, the dog is intelligent and loyal and makes a good companion and watchdog.

It may be small, but the Tibetan Spaniel carries itself with pride. But don't be fooled: it also has an exuberant side to its nature and loves to play. Loyal to its family but aloof with strangers, it makes an excellent watchdog.

TIBETAN TERRIER

The breed has a history stretching back over 2,000 years, and in its native lands was thought to bring luck to its owner as well as having religious associations; in fact, the Tibetan Terrier is also known as the Holy Dog. Although the word 'terrier' is in its name, it is actually a herding dog, and often accompanied traders travelling to and from China.

A well-built, long-coated dog reminiscent of a small Old English Sheepdog. The head has a medium-length skull and a strong muzzle. The nose is black. The round, dark-brown eyes are large and set widely apart. The V-shaped ears are pendent and heavily feathered. The neck is of medium length and is carried on a compact and well-muscled body. The legs are well-boned, terminating in large, round feet. The well-plumed tail is carried curled over the back.

The outercoat is profuse, fine and long; it may be straight or waved, but not curled. The undercoat is fine and woolly. Colours are white, cream,

golden, smoke, grey, black, parti-colour or tricolour.

This is the largest of the Tibetan breeds in the utility group. An energetic and enthusiastic dog, the Tibetan Terrier is friendly towards those it knows, being loyal and full of character. The dog makes a good pet and will eagerly guard both the house and the family within.

The Tibetan Terrier is the largest of the Tibetan breeds, and is associated with good luck. It is bursting with energy, and requires regular play sessions in oder to maintain its zest for life.

Chapter Five
GUN DOGS

Dogs in this group were all bred to assist in the hunting and retrieval of game. As early as the 6th century BC, records existed of certain types of dog which, instead of pursuing game, sniffed the air with raised head, then stood completely still. Although considered a rather unsatisfactory characteristic in a hunting dog, it was later realized that this could in fact be useful behaviour, given the right circumstances, such as when hunters wanted to net partridge or quail, for example. So the dogs were trained to crouch, sit, or lie down once they had spotted the game, leaving the hunters to draw nets over the birds before they could fly away.

This is the origin of the name 'bird dog', although most gun dogs today are employed in helping to hunt furred quarry as well as the feathered variety. After the invention of the gun, and perhaps in recognition of the wider role played by the dog, the name bird dog was changed to the more appropriate gun dog.

A gun dog works in several ways: first, it must search around to locate the whereabouts of the quarry by scent. Then it indicates the quarry's location by standing in full view of it and pointing – in other words, adopting a motionless stance indicating the position of the game. Next, the gun dog must move forward to put the game up, which means causing the bird or other quarry to move

from cover so that the hunter can shoot it. Lastly, the gun dog must retrieve the prey without damaging it further.

Among the features exhibited by gun dogs are weatherproof coats that enable them to work often in cold, wet, conditions, including freezing water. In order to respond consistently and obediently to commands, gun dogs must be loyal, willing to please, and friendly by nature – features that make this group the most popular of all in terms of them being pets and companions for human beings. The stealthy nature of their work also means that gun dogs are less given to vocalization than hounds; again, a considerable attribute in a house dog.

Field trials are held regularly in which the qualities of the various types of gun dogs are tested, and certain characteristics thought to be necessary for field work, such as speed or stamina, are then bred on. Sometimes these same features are considered less important in the show dog – where appearance may be more highly prized – which explains the divergence that often occurs between the

OPPOSITE: A willing, merry dog, the Cocker Spaniel has all the attributes of a well-balanced sporting dog. It enjoys company and exercise and likes carrying things around in its mouth.

RIGHT: The Labrador Retriever is intelligent, soft-mouthed, and displays a willingness to work and a love of water. Happiest out in the countryside, the dog nevertheless makes an adaptable and devoted family pet, being especially patient with children.

working dog and the show dog of the same breed.

Among the gun dogs, different breeds are used for the various tasks in the field. The gun dogs that exhibit pointing behaviour include such breeds as the English and German Pointers and the English Setter, while dogs such as the Springer Spaniel are prized for their ability to flush game from cover. Some dogs will also be expected to retrieve as well, the best-known of the retrieving breeds being the Golden Retriever and the Flat-Coated Retriever.

Some are bred to participate in all aspects of hunting. This is particularly the case in mainland Europe, where such dogs are known as Hunt, Point and Retrieve (HPR) breeds. These include the Weimaraner from Germany, the Large Münsterlander (also from Germany), and the Italian Spinone.

BRACCO ITALIANO

This is a breed of dog developed in Italy as a versatile gun dog. It is common in its native land, but rare elsewhere. The Bracco Italiano is the result of matings between gun dogs and hounds in the 18th century to produce a dog with the best characteristics of both types – in other words, a pointing type of dog with additional stamina. This is one of a number of similar multi-purpose dogs, which have become popular in Europe as Hunt, Point and Retrieve (HPR) breeds.

A robust, lean and muscular dog with a long and angular head, the skull is broad, and the muzzle is long and deep. The nose is flesh-coloured or chestnut, and the eyes range from yellow to brown. The ears are long and pendulous. The short and powerful neck is carried on a deep-chested body with a strong back. Long, well-muscled legs terminate in sturdy, oval feet. The medium-length tail may be docked. The gait should be long and fluid, with plenty of reach and drive. The head should be held above the topline.

The coat is fine, dense and glossy. Colours are orange-and-white, orange roan, chestnut-and-white or chestnut roan.

The Bracco Italiano is a powerful and hard-working dog with something of the Bloodhound in its makeup. It is friendly and docile and its fine coat is easy to keep clean.

The Bracco Italiano has a docile, friendly nature, despite its multiple role as hunter, pointer and retriever.

A vigorous hunter, the Brittany is as famous for its charm as it is for its abilities in the field.

The Brittany has a flat, dense, fine wavy coat. Colours are orange-and-white, liver-and-white, black-and-white, tricolour or a roan of any of these colours.

This active and energetic dog is keen to please and therefore easy to train. A good worker in the field, with the ability to hunt, point and retrieve, the Brittany is both intelligent and affectionate.

BRITTANY

Coming from France, the Brittany is another Hunt, Point and Retrieve breed. The dog was once known as the Brittany Spaniel, and although this is a true French spaniel, it is really more like a small setter. These good-natured and friendly dogs have gained popularity in America and will likely increase their fan club in Britain, too.

A compact and square-looking dog with a medium-length skull and a well-defined stop. The muzzle is tapered. The expressive eyes are brown, harmonizing with the coat-colour. The drop ears are set high and are rather short. The medium-length neck is carried on a deep-chested body with a short, slightly sloping back. The legs are quite well-boned, long and muscular, and the feet are small. These dogs are often born without tails, but when tails are present they are short or may be docked.

ENGLISH SETTER

One of the oldest gun dog breeds, and also one of the most stylish and admired, the English Setter shows evidence of a mixed ancestry involving pointers and spaniels. Development of the breed into the animal recognized today began in the mid 19th century, and came largely from stock that had been kept pure for over 35 years.

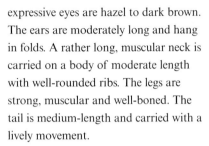

Animals from this line were mixed with others to produce dogs with temperaments better suited for hunting.

The English Setter is a dog with clean, elegant lines and a smooth movement. The head is long with a moderately broad skull and a moderately deep and square muzzle. The nose should be black or liver, depending on the coat-colour. The bright, expressive eyes are hazel to dark brown. The ears are moderately long and hang in folds. A rather long, muscular neck is carried on a body of moderate length with well-rounded ribs. The legs are strong, muscular and well-boned. The tail is medium-length and carried with a lively movement.

The coat is wavy, long and silky; shorter on the head, and with a well-feathered tail, breeches and fore legs. Colours are black-and-white (known as blue belton), orange-and-white (known as orange belton), lemon-and-white (known as lemon belton), liver-and-white (known as liver belton) or tricolour (known as blue-belton-and-tan, or liver-belton-and-tan).

A dog that excels at its task in the field, quartering the ground at speed and then setting rapidly when the quarry is located. This breed also makes a first-rate companion and pet, being active and ready to play, but may need firm handling. As with most long-coated breeds, it takes time to get the dog ready for the house after a day spent out in the fields.

The elegant English Setter is the oldest of the gun dogs, and seems to have an innate sense of what is expected of it in the field. As a pet, however, it has a tendency to roam and needs a good deal of exercise.

GERMAN SHORTHAIRED POINTER

The origins of the breed probably stem from stock owned by Prince Albert zu Somsbrauenfels, which although worthy were rather slow German gun dogs. These were crossed with English Pointers, combining the excellent scenting abilities of the German dogs with the more spirited English qualities to produce a highly versatile Hunt, Point and Retrieve gun dog.

The German Shorthaired Pointer is a well-balanced animal displaying power, endurance and symmetry. The head is lean and clean-cut with a broad skull and a long, strong muzzle. The nose is solid brown or black, depending on the coat-colour. The brown eyes are medium-sized, with a soft but intelligent expression. The moderately long ears hang down flat. A fairly long neck is carried on a deep-chested body with a firm, short back and slightly arched loins. The legs are strong and well-boned. The tail is usually docked to a medium length.

The coat is short, dense and flat. Colours are solid black or solid liver, and both coat-colours may be spotted or ticked with white.

This is an aristocratic-looking dog that gives an impression of alertness and energy, being a dual-purpose

pointer/retriever with a keen nose and great perseverance in the field. Rippling with muscular power, this is a dog that needs plenty of regular exercise. It is also loyal, gentle and affectionate as well as being easy to train.

The handsome German Shorthaired Pointer is the older type and is a versatile all-rounder in the field. It makes a good pet but is happier when it has plenty of work to do.

GERMAN WIREHAIRED POINTER

Created by selectively breeding certain German gun dog breeds with the German Shorthair, this attractive and hardy character is a little bigger than its shorthaired cousin, and is another Hunt, Point and Retrieve breed.

The head is moderately long with a broad skull. The nose is liver or black. The medium-sized oval eyes are hazel or a darker shade. The medium-sized, rounded ears hang down. A strong neck is carried on a deep-chested body with a firm back that falls slightly towards the rear. The legs are strong and muscular. The tail is customarily docked to a medium length, and is held horizontally when on the move.

The outercoat is harsh, thick and weather-resistant; the undercoat is dense. Bushy eyebrows and a full beard

are desirable features. Colours are liver-and-white, liver, or black-and-white.

This is a strong, wirehaired hunting breed, equally capable of working in water as over ground. An alert, intelligent and steady dog, it is also loyal and affectionate and good in the house. Being essentially a working breed, however, it will require plenty of regular exercise.

The German Wirehaired Pointer is a robust hunting dog, happy to work in water and over any other terrain. It has a tendency to pick quarrels with other dogs, but is generally good with people and reliable where children are concerned.

GORDON SETTER

As its name implies, the Gordon Setter is of Scottish origin and was bred to perfection by the Duke of Gordon in the late 18th century. Because the breed is somewhat less fashionable than the Irish or English Setters, the Gordon Setter has remained a no-nonsense, steady, working gun dog, capable of going all day if necessary.

This is a well-built, stylish-looking dog with a glossy coat. The head is deeper than it is broad, with a moderately broad skull and a long, almost square-ended muzzle. The nose is black. The eyes are dark brown and intelligent-looking. The ears are medium-length and pendulous. The neck is long, carried on a short, deep body with slightly arched loins. Strong, moderately-long, well-boned legs terminate in oval feet. The tail is long and tapers to the tip.

The coat should be soft and glossy, straight or slightly wavy. The hair on the ears, beneath the stomach, on the

chest, back of legs and under the tail is long. Colour is coal-black with tan markings of a rich, chestnut red.

The Gordon Setter is heavier and less fleet of foot than the English or Irish Setters. But it is a bold, outgoing dog, being capable, trustworthy and intelligent with an even disposition. The coat needs regular grooming to maintain its high gloss.

Because the Gordon Setter has never been as fashionable as the English and the Irish Setter (pictured to the far right of the picture on the left), it has remained true to type. A natural pointer and retriever, the Gordon also makes a delightful pet, but tends to be more reserved with strangers.

HUNGARIAN VIZSLA

A native of the plains of central Hungary, the Vizsla is also sometimes called the Hungarian Pointer. The breed suffered as a result of wars in 20th-century Europe, but it was rescued from the point of extinction to become a first-class gun dog – particularly capable in water – and to enjoy considerable show success in Britain and America.

Medium-sized and of a particularly distinctive and powerful appearance, the head is lean and muscular, with a moderately long skull and muzzle. The nose is brown. The slightly oval eyes should tone in colour with the coat. The ears are fairly large, rounded V-shapes and hang down. The neck is moderately long and muscular. The back is short and well-muscled, and the chest is moderately deep. The legs are fairly long and well-boned. The tail is fairly thick, and is customarily docked to two-thirds of its length.

The coat is short, smooth, dense and glossy. The colour is a rusty gold.

A lively and intelligent dog with great stamina, the Hungarian Vizsla is an excellent general-purpose gun dog, combining a good nose with stable pointing and reliable retrieving skills. The breed also makes a gentle, affectionate and protective pet, and can adapt itself to all kinds of homes.

Also known as the Hungarian Pointer, the Vizsla is very good at jumping, besides being a talented swimmer, and will easily scale a fence if it is not built high enough to contain it.

HUNGARIAN WIREHAIRED VIZSLA

A close relative of the smooth-coated Hungarian Vizsla (see opposite), the Wirehaired Vizsla was produced by crossing the former with rough-coated dogs of German origin. The resulting Wirehaired Vizsla's rough coat therefore affords the dog more protection during winter, when it is often required to wait in boats and to retrieve game from cold water.

The head is lean and distinguished-looking, with a moderately wide skull and a tapering but well-squared muzzle. The soft brown eyes and bushy, bearded face give the dog an appealing quality. The nose is brown. The eyes should be a shade darker than the coat. The fairly low-set ears are rounded V-shapes. The moderately-long, muscular neck is carried on a well-muscled body with a short back and high withers. The moderately-long legs are well-boned.

The tail is customarily docked to two-thirds of its length and is carried horizontally when on the move.

The coat is dense and rough, lying close to the body, being shorter on the ears, head and legs; a beard and pronounced eyebrows are desirable. Coat-colour is a russet gold.

A hard-working HPR breed of striking appearance. Lively, intelligent and easy to train, the dog is also endearingly affectionate and protective towards its owner.

The Hungarian Wirehaired Viszla adapts well to urban living but requires plenty of space. It can be destructive when bored.

IRISH RED-AND-WHITE SETTER

A close relative of the Irish Setter and arising from similar stock, one of the most famous owners of these dogs was Lord Rossmore of Monaghan, and for this reason the breed is sometimes known as the Rossmore Setter. The dog is similar in build to the Irish Setter but is altogether heavier and with a more powerful, broader head. Now gaining in popularity, the Irish Red-and-White Setter is a truly striking dog.

Athletic and powerful, the head is broad in proportion to the body, with a well-defined stop. The skull is domed and the muzzle is square. The round eyes are hazel to dark brown. The ears are set well back and lie close to the head. The very muscular neck is carried

on a strong, muscular body with a deep chest. The legs are strong and well-muscled. A well-feathered tail is carried level with the back, or slightly below, when the dog is on the move.

Fine texture, coupled with good feathering, are features of the Irish Red-and-White Setter's coat. The coat should not be curly, although slight waviness is permitted. The base colour should be white, with solid red patches. Some mottling on the face, feet and lower parts of the legs is permitted.

This is a friendly and obedient dog that proves itself equally well out in the field as it does in the home.

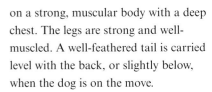

The good-looking Irish Red-and-White Setter has most of the characteristics of the Irish Setter but with distinctive red-and-white markings. It needs plenty of exercise in order to thrive.

IRISH SETTER

This is one of the most glamorous of the breeds, with its striking chestnut coat. The dashing Irish Setter, often called the Red Setter, began to increase in popularity from the late 1800s, although little is known concerning the true origins of the breed.

This is a sleek and handsome dog with a racy appearance. The head is long and lean, with a fairly narrow, oval skull and a long, almost square muzzle. The nose is dark brown to black. The kindly-looking eyes are dark brown. The ears are of medium length, hanging in neat folds close to the head. The muscular neck is carried on a deep-chested, rather narrow body. The legs are fairly long and strongly boned. The tail should be fairly long and in proportion with the body size; it is carried level with the back, or just below, when on the move.

The coat is of a moderate length, flat, and free from curl or waviness if possible, being short and fine on the head, front of legs, and ear-tips, with feathering on the upper parts of the ears and backs of legs; there is longer

The Irish Setter is very popular as a pet, being friendly and spirited, but it must not be forgotten that it is an active and able working dog and needs plenty of space to run free.

hair on belly and tail. Colour is a rich chestnut red with no traces of black.

Despite the Irish Setter's refined appearance, this is an active, willing and able sporting dog, with a carefree disposition, although more training is normally required than for other setters to ensure obedience. The breed is also hugely popular as a pet, thanks to its affectionate and playful nature. The coat needs plenty of attention to maintain its sleek, healthy appearance.

ITALIAN SPINONE

One of the many Continental HPR breeds, the Italian Spinone has a very ancient ancestry, comprising native Italian hounds crossed with French Griffons among others. The Spinone is mostly used for hunting in woodland and in marshy terrain. The breed only achieved championship status in Britain in 1994, but in a relatively short time has achieved a well-deserved popularity.

A solid-looking dog with a benign expression, the head is long with a flattish skull and a squarish muzzle. The large eyes are yellow, orange or ochre depending on the coat-colour. The triangular ears are pendulous and covered with short, thick hair. The neck is strong and short. The body is short

and deep with a broad chest. The legs are long and well-boned. The tail is thick but is usually docked to half its length.

The coat is thick and close-lying, being slightly tough and wiry; eyebrows, moustache and beard are pronounced. Colours are white, or white with orange or chestnut patches or spots.

The Italian Spinone is a strong, all-purpose gun dog with a willing and capable disposition. It also makes a trustworthy and affectionate family pet.

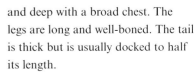

The Italian Spinone is a relative newcomer to the showing world. It also has an amiable disposition that makes it a good pet.

KOOIKERHONDJE

A small breed from the Netherlands, the Kooikerhondje is used for helping to trap swimming ducks in nets. It is a fairly new arrival to the international show scene.

An attractive, medium-sized dog with a flowing coat. The moderate-sized skull and muzzle are approximately equal in length, and the nose is black. The eyes are dark brown, giving an impression of alertness. The medium-sized ears are pendulous with long feathering. A short, muscular neck is carried on a strong body with a level back and a deep chest. The legs are strong and partly feathered, terminating in hare-like feet. The tail is well-feathered and carried level with the back, or slightly higher, when the dog is on the move.

The Kooikerhondje has a medium-length, slightly wavy or straight outercoat, close-fitting and with a well-developed undercoat. Colour consists of red-orange patches on a white background; a white blaze is desirable.

This is a compact, energetic dog, with a happy, friendly and affectionate disposition.

The Dutch Kooikerhondje is an excellent swimmer, used for herding ducks into nets. It is a friendly and energetic little dog.

LARGE MÜNSTERLANDER

The Large Münsterlander originated in Münster, Germany, and was developed after the First World War from the same stock that was used to create the similar-looking Small Münsterlander.

The Large Münsterlander is a distinctive, muscular dog with an alert expression. The head is lean, the skull is moderately-broad, and the muzzle is long. The nose is black, and the eyes are dark brown with an intelligent expression. The ears hang flat, and their covering of hair should extend beyond the tips. The neck is strong and muscular, sitting on a body with a strong back and a wide chest. The back is slightly higher at the shoulders. The legs are well-muscled. The tail tapers towards the tip and, these days, is rarely docked.

The dog has a long, thick coat, shorter on the head but well-feathered on the fore legs, hind legs and tail. The head should be solid black in colour, although a white blaze or star is

permitted; the body is white with large black patches, flecks, or ticking.

Easily trained and a good worker with an energetic, easy movement, the Large Münsterlander is adaptable in all kinds of terrain, including water. The breed also makes an ideal family companion, being loyal, affectionate and patient with children.

The Large Münsterlander is equally at home working over rough terrain and water as it is as a family pet. An attractive dog, it is both intelligent and loyal.

NOVA SCOTIA DUCK-TOLLING RETRIEVER

Of Canadian origin, where it was selectively bred with an emphasis on intelligence, the first examples of the breed arrived in Britain in 1988. In the field, the dog's role is to wave its abundant, white-tipped tail to attract ducks and other waterfowl to within range of the hunters' guns, and then to retrieve any kills.

This is a richly-coloured dog of compact and powerful appearance. The skull is wedge-shaped, broad and slightly rounded, and the muzzle tapers from stop to nose. The nose may be black or flesh-coloured. The medium-sized eyes are brown or amber. The triangular-shaped ears are held slightly erect at their bases. The neck is of moderate length and well-muscled. The deep-chested body has a short back and strong, muscular loins. The legs are strong and muscular and terminate in round, strongly webbed feet – an adaptation for swimming. The tail is well-feathered and curled over the back when the dog is alert.

The dog has a medium-length double coat with a softer undercoat. The hair is straight and water-repellent. There is feathering on the throat, behind the ears, at the back of the thighs, and on the fore legs.

Colour may be any shade of orange or red, with lighter tail feathering; white tips to the tail, feet and chest are permitted.

A powerful swimmer and tracker, the Nova Scotia Duck-Tolling Retriever, or Duck-Toller as it is often known, also makes a playful and friendly pet.

A most attractive dog with a rich, waterproof coat and powerful build. The Nova Scotia Duck-Tolling Retriever, or Duck-Toller as it is also known, is perfectly at home in water and has webbed feet that enhance its already effective swimming capabilities.

POINTER

The Pointer is thought to have originated in Spain, but was used in Britain from the mid 17th century to indicate, by pointing, where game was lying up. In the early 18th century, when guns came into more general use, the Pointer was further bred to improve its ability as a gun dog. The traits exhibited by the modern-day Pointer are excellent scenting powers, a speedy action over the ground, and a steadiness when pointing.

The breed should give the impression of compact power, agility, and alertness. The head is aristocratic, with a moderately-broad skull and a long muzzle with a concave nose bridge. The eyes, which should have a kindly expression, are brown or hazel, according to the coat-colour. The ears are medium-length and hang down. The neck is long, round and strong. The body is short and fairly broad with a deep chest, carried on moderately-long, strongly boned legs. The tail is medium length, swinging from side to side when the dog is on the move.

The coat is short, fine and hard with a sheen. Colours are lemon-and-

white, orange-and-white, liver-and-white and black-and-white. Solid colours and tricolours are also permitted.

The Pointer is an enthusiastic and able worker, endowed with qualities of speed and endurance. It also adapts well to family life, being docile, intelligent and affectionate.

These versatile, athletic dogs are excellent all-rounders, able to perform all the duties required of a gun dog in the field. They are not only well-behaved in the home, but they also make effective watchdogs.

CHESAPEAKE BAY RETRIEVER

During the early part of the 19th century two puppies, reported as Newfoundland in type, were rescued from a shipwreck off the coast of Maryland, USA. The dogs were mated with local retrievers, these crossings being the start of the breed known as the Chesapeake Bay Retriever.

The dog was used to retrieve ducks from the cold waters of Chesapeake Bay, it being suitably adapted for this purpose by virtue of its thick, oily, waterproof coat. A layer of subcutaneous fat also helped to keep out the cold and added to the dog's overall impression of solidity.

A strong, muscular dog with a distinctive coat, the skull is broad with a shortish, relatively broad muzzle. The nose-colour should harmonize with the coat. The eyes should be yellow or amber. The small ears hang loosely at the sides of the head. The muscular neck tapers from the head to the shoulders. The body is of medium length with a deep chest. The strong,

medium-length legs terminate in webbed hare-like feet. The tail is heavy and strong, straight or slightly curved.

The coat is short and thick with a dense, woolly undercoat. The coat should be oily and able to resist water. Any colour ranging from dark brown to faded tan or the colour of dead grass is permitted.

Essentially a duck dog, and in its element when working in water, the Chesapeake Bay Retriever is willing, courageous and independent. It also makes a good guardian and companion – albeit one with a very hearty appetite.

The Chesapeake is a hardy, outdoor type and probably the most talented of the duck dogs. It has the uncanny ability to remember where each duck falls and to retrieve it swiftly.

CURLY-COATED RETRIEVER

The breed arose as the result of crossings between water spaniels, various sorts of retrievers and, possibly, pointers. The tight, curly coat was probably enhanced by adding poodle stock to the breeding programme. The breed reached the peak of its popularity in the latter half of the 19th century, when many were taken to Australia and New Zealand to be used for hunting birds. The unique coat is well-adapted for work in water and is suitably quick-drying.

A strong, elegant-looking dog with a dark, curly coat. The head is long and wedge-shaped with a fairly broad skull and longish muzzle. The nose is black in dogs with black fur and brown in brown-coated dogs. The eyes are large and again should harmonize with the coat-colour. The pendulous ears are rather small and lie close to the head. The strong neck is carried on a broad body with a deep chest. The legs are strong and muscular and terminate in round feet. The tail is long.

The coat is a mass of small, tight curls extending over most of the body

except for the face and skull. Colours are black or liver.

In the field, the Curly-Coated Retriever is adept at marking where fallen game is lying and retrieving it. An intelligent dog with great stamina and confidence, the breed is happiest when leading an active life in the open – preferably around water. It is a friendly and loyal dog.

The Curly-Coated Retriever is the result of crossing water spaniels, retrievers and poodles to produce the distinctive curly coat. The dog is at its happiest doing the job for which it was bred.

FLAT-COATED RETRIEVER

A blend of the St John's Newfoundland (a smaller version of the Newfoundland) and spaniels, setters and sheepdogs, the breed was first shown in Britain in 1859. For some years the Flat-Coated Retriever as been less popular than other types of gun dog, but there is now a growing interest in the breed, which has the lightest build of all the retrievers.

This is a medium-sized dog with an intelligent expression and an active nature. The head is long, with a medium to broad skull and a longish muzzle. The eyes are dark brown to hazel. The ears are small and close-fitting to the sides of the head. The

body has a rather broad, deep chest. Moderately-long, strongly boned legs terminate in rounded feet with thick pads. The tail is fairly short and carried jauntily, but seldom above the level of the back.

The coat is dense, of a fine to medium texture, and should be as flat as possible. Colours are black or liver.

The Flat-Coated Retriever matures slowly, retaining its puppy-like quality for years. This is a cheerful, playful extrovert that enjoys the companionship of human beings, yet makes a good guard dog when required. In the field, the dog works effectively and it is a capable and enthusiasic swimmer.

A keen and proficient swimmer, the Flat-Coated Retriever is also naturally playful, behaving like a puppy well into adulthood, with the result that it is late to mature.

GOLDEN RETRIEVER

Thought to have stemmed from the initial crossing of a yellow wavy-coated retriever with a spaniel, before mating on with setters and other retrievers, these dogs were first known as Retrievers (Golden or Yellow), but in 1920 assumed their present name. One of the most versatile of breeds, and also one of the most popular, the Golden Retriever is used to retrieve game in the field, for detecting drugs and explosives, as a tracker and guide dog – and last but not least as a favourite family pet.

The head has a broad skull with a powerful, wide and deep muzzle. The nose should be black, and the eyes are dark brown and have a kindly expression. Ears are moderately large and hang flat to the head. A clean, muscular neck is carried on a shortish body with deep ribs. The legs are fairly long and well-boned, terminating in round, cat-like feet. The muscular tail is carried level with the back; it is used for steering when swimming.

The coat can be flat or wavy but well-feathered; the undercoat is dense and water-resistant. Colour may be any shade of cream or gold.

An intelligent dog that is easy to train. The breed is of a confident, friendly and patient temperament and makes an enthusiastic pet – wagging its tail with vigour to express its pleasure.

Its intelligence and even temperament make the Golden Retriever one of the most versatile of dogs – used to retrieve game in the field, for detecting drugs and explosives, as a tracker and guide dog, and as a favourite family pet.

LABRADOR RETRIEVER

Believed to have its origins in Greenland, where similar dogs were once used by fishermen to retrieve fish. It was introduced to Britain in the late 1800s, where it earned a good reputation in field trials. The breed club for these dogs was begun comparatively recently, in 1916, with the Yellow Labrador club being formed in 1925. One the best-known and popular breeds in the world today, the Labrador Retriever is a great all-rounder, in that it can be utilized in a variety of working roles as well as that of a companion and pet.

Instantly recognizable, the overall impression is of a strongly-built, active dog. The head has a broad skull with a broad, medium-length muzzle. The eyes are brown or hazel, and should express intelligence and good nature. The ears are set fairly far back on the head and hang flat. The strong neck is carried on a body with a broad, deep chest. The legs are well-developed. The tail is thick and broad and covered in short, dense fur, giving the dog a rounded look.

The distinctive outercoat is short and dense and fairly hard to the touch; the undercoat is waterproof. Colours may be solid black, yellow or liver.

The Labrador is an intelligent, soft-mouthed retriever with a willingness to work and a love of water. Happiest out in the countryside, the dog nevertheless makes an adaptable and devoted family pet and is patient with children.

Labradors are capable, energetic dogs, eager and enthusiastic to work and play. Beware of overfeeding, however, for there is also a tendency towards obesity.

AMERICAN COCKER SPANIEL

This attractive-looking long-coated dog was bred in America in the 19th century from Cocker Spaniels imported from Britain, its main job being to retrieve gamebirds such as quail. The smallest in the gun dog group, the American Cocker is a sound and willing worker, but is today more often seen in the show ring or family home than working in the field.

A distinctive, smallish, neat dog with a full coat on the legs and abdomen. The head is shortish and refined, with a rounded skull and a deep, broad muzzle. The nose should be black in black-and-tans and brown or black in dogs of other colours. The eyes are full and round, with a forward-looking gaze; the expression should be alert and appealing. The ears are long and lobe-shaped and should be covered in long fur. The neck is long and muscular. The body is short and compact with a deep chest; the back slopes slightly from withers to tail. The legs are strong and muscular. The tail is usually docked by three-fifths of its length.

The medium-length coat is silky and flat or slightly wavy, shorter on the

head. The dog comes in various colours including solid black and black-and-tan.

A keen and happy dog with a friendly and confident manner, the American Cocker makes an excellent family pet, although the luxuriant coat needs to be regularly groomed.

Derived from the same stock as its English cousin, the American Cocker Spaniel has evolved so differently that it is now recognized as a separate breed. It is the smallest of the gun dog breeds, used to retrieve gamebirds. Now, however, it is more often regarded as an appealing family pet.

CLUMBER SPANIEL

Believed to have originated by crossing a spaniel of some type with a Basset, the breed was brought to Britain by a French duke at the beginning of the French Revolution and thereafter remained safely at Clumber Park, the Duke of Newcastle's family seat, which is how the name arose. By the late 1850s, the Clumber Spaniel was being shown and today it is a highly-valued retriever.

A distinctive, massively-built dog with a thoughtful expression. The Clumber moves with the rolling gait characteristic of the breed. The head is massive with a fairly broad skull and a heavy, square muzzle with well-developed flews. The eyes should be dark amber, slightly sunk, and showing a moderate amount of haw. The ears are described as resembling vine leaves and hang slightly forward. The neck is thick and powerful. The body is long, heavy and deep and close to the ground; the loins are muscular. The legs are short and well-developed. The tail is low-set and carried level with the back when on the move.

The abundant coat is close, silky and straight. The legs, chest and tail are well-feathered. The colour is plain-white with lemon (preferably) or orange patches.

A steady and intelligent dog with a good nose, the Clumber Spaniel makes a dignified companion for a country-dweller.

The Clumber Spaniel is best suited to life in the country and is highly valued as a retriever.

ENGLISH COCKER SPANIEL

One of the oldest spaniel breeds, the dog's original name of Cocking Spaniel derived from it being used to flush woodcocks from cover in woods and marshes. The Cocker was recognized as a separate breed from Springer and Field Spaniels soon after the UK Kennel Club was formed in 1873. Cockers used for work are less sturdy and less heavy than their counterparts in the show ring. This is the most popular of the spaniel breeds.

The overall impression is of a merry, compact, well-balanced sporting dog. The skull should be not too broad

or long, and the muzzle should be square with a distinct stop. The eyes are dark brown, a lighter brown, or hazel, toning with the coat; the expression is intelligent, alert and gentle. The ears are lobe-shaped, thin and pendulous. A muscular, moderate-length neck is carried on a strong, compact body with a well-developed chest. The legs are short and strongly boned, ending in cat-like feet. The tail is usually docked, but never so short that it impedes its non-stop action when the dog is moving.

The coat is flat and silky, with well-feathered fore legs, hind legs (above the hocks) and body. Various colours are permitted; self-colours should only have white on the chest.

A willing and happy dog if ever there was one, the Cocker is quick to adapt to its surroundings and is equally at home sniffing around outdoors as it is playing inside the house with its family. The breed enjoys exercise and company and loves carrying things about in its mouth.

The Cocker has charm matched with good looks and a lively personality. It needs all the exercise you can give it, but be sure to remove tangles from the coat after a walk in the woods.

ENGLISH SPRINGER SPANIEL

Formerly known as the Norfolk Spaniel, this pure and ancient breed was awarded official status in 1902. The breed gets the name 'springer' from the fact that it was used to flush birds into the air from cover so that they would spring upwards and thus be bagged.

The English Springer is a compact, racy dog of symmetrical build that stands high on the leg. The medium-length skull is fairly broad, and the muzzle is rather broad and deep. The almond-shaped eyes, of hazel coloration, have a kind and alert expression. The ears are lobe-shaped, fairly long, and hang flat to the head.

The neck is rather long, strong and muscular. The body is strong with a deep chest and is carried on well-developed legs. The tail, customarily docked, is well-feathered and has a lively action.

The long, dense and soft coat is also tough and weather-resistant, with feathering on the ears, fore legs, belly and hindquarters. Colours are black-and-white, liver-and-white, or these colours with tan markings.

This is a friendly, extrovert gun dog, willing to search for, flush, and retrieve game – even in icy water. It is an affectionate family dog, but one that needs plenty of exercise.

Formerly known as the Norfolk Spaniel, the Springer is an ancient breed. It excels in the field, flushing out game, but as a pet needs plenty of space in which to run and swim to prevent it from getting lazy and obese.

FIELD SPANIEL

The breed arose through crossings between Sussex and Cocker Spaniels, but the Field Spaniel has enjoyed mixed fortunes: the breed almost disappeared in the early 1900s and again in the 1950s. At one time, its numbers were so small that the Kennel Club would not allow it championship status, although determined efforts by enthusiasts and breeders were able to reverse this decision in the 1960s.

Built for activity and endurance and one with a noble character, the head has a broad, long skull and a lean muzzle. The almond-shaped eyes are dark hazel in colour and have a gentle expression. The moderately-long ears are set low and are well-feathered. The neck is long and muscular. The body has a level, strong back and a deep chest. The moderate-length legs terminate in round feet. The tail is docked by one-third and should not be carried higher than the back.

The Field Spaniel has a coat which is flat, glossily silky, weatherproof and dense, being well-feathered on the chest, underbody and behind the legs. Colours are black, liver, golden-liver, mahogany or roan; any of these colours with tan markings are permissible.

White or roan is permissible on the chest of solid-coloured dogs.

An active gun dog, but one that is also placid, obedient and intelligent. The breed is not recommended for the town-dweller, however, since the Field Spaniel really belongs where its name suggests – out in the open countryside.

The Field Spaniel is a working dog through and through, as its name suggests. It is in its true element out in the countryside, and could never be entirely happy living in town.

IRISH WATER SPANIEL

This is a very ancient breed, but there is some disagreement among experts as to its true ancestry. What is undeniable, however, is that the Water Spaniel is a versatile worker in the field as well as being a good companion. This is the tallest of the spaniel breeds.

A large and purposeful-looking spaniel with a distinctive curly coat. The skull is high-domed and fairly broad and long, and the muzzle is long and strong. The nose is dark liver in colour. The eyes have an alert expression and are amber to dark brown. The long ears are oval-shaped and pendulous. The neck is powerful and arching and is carried on a short, deep body. The legs are long and strongly boned and terminate in large feet. The tail is fairly long and tapers to a point.

The coat is composed of dense, crisp, tight ringlets and has a natural oiliness that repels moisture when the dog is retrieving from water; the coat is

shorter on the muzzle, throat and lower part of the tail. Coat-colour is a rich, dark liver.

This is a useful gun dog, especially when retrieving from water is required. Although sometimes described as reserved, the dog is affectionate and faithful, and fans of the breed talk of its great sense of humour. Thorough grooming is required.

The Irish Water Spaniel is excellent at retrieving and even better where water in involved, hence its name. It makes a good pet, but the curly coat requires regular attention.

SUSSEX SPANIEL

Like the Field Spaniel, the Sussex is a breed rarely seen today, being seemingly less fashionable than the more lightly-built spaniel breeds. In fact, the Sussex Spaniel is a heavily-built dog with a characteristic rolling gait when on the move. The breed first arose in Sussex, England, over 120 years ago.

A massive and powerfully-built dog with a heavy-browed expression. The head is medium to long with a broad skull and a long, square muzzle. The nose is liver. The large hazel eyes have a gentle expression. The ears are thick and lobular and hang flat to the head. The neck is long and strong and is carried on a deep and muscular body. The well-boned legs are rather short. The tail is usually docked and has a lively action.

The Sussex Spaniel has an abundant, flat coat with good feathering on the forequarters and hindquarters. Colour is golden-liver.

The Sussex is unusual among spaniels in being more vocal when at work. It is also energetic, despite its heavy appearance, and is quite docile and friendly.

The Sussex Spaniel is a rare sight these days. It is a powerful dog with a strange rolling action when on the move. It is also different from other spaniels in that it is vocal when working.

WELSH SPRINGER SPANIEL

Red-and-white spaniels closely resembling the Welsh have existed for many years. The Welsh Springer Spaniel was recognized by the Kennel Club in 1902. Slightly lighter in build than the English Springer, the Welsh was used extensively for hunting but is nowadays seen increasingly at shows.

A compact and attractively marked dog, similar to but slightly smaller than the English Springer. The head has a moderate-length, slightly domed skull and a medium-length muzzle. The nose is flesh-coloured or darker. The eyes are hazel or dark brown with a kindly expression. The ears are fairly small and hang flat to the head. The neck is long and muscular. The body is not very long but is strong and muscular. Medium-length, well-boned legs terminate in round, cat-like feet. The tail is usually docked and has a lively action.

The coat is straight, thick and silky; feathering occurs on the fore legs, hind legs above the hocks, ears and tail. Colour is rich red-and-white.

Fast and active, this is a dog built to work hard without tiring. It also makes an obedient and friendly household pet.

The attractively marked Welsh Springer Spaniel is slighter and smaller than its English counterpart. It is extremely agile and it is able to work fast without tiring.

WEIMARANER

The Weimaraner gets its name from the German court of Weimar, where the dog was very popular. Dogs of similar appearance, albeit more hound-like, appear in paintings from the early 1600s by Van Dyck. The dog has proved effective performing HPR duties. Originally it was used to hunt boar and deer, but today it usually accompanies hunters looking for smaller game. The most commonly seen version of this dog is the shorthaired variety, although there is also a longhaired form.

A tall, elegant and purposeful-looking dog with unusual coloration. The head is fairly long and aristocratic with a long muzzle. The nose is grey. The eyes are round and vary in colour

from amber to blue-grey. The ears are long, taper to a point, and are slightly folded. A moderately-long neck is carried on a rather long body with a deep chest, and the legs are strong and well-boned. The tail is docked.

The coat is short and sleek. In the longhaired variety, the fur is 1–2in (2.5–5cm) long, with feathering on the tail and the back of the limbs. Colour is silver grey, mouse grey or roe grey, all with a metallic sheen.

An able multi-role hunting dog which is fearless but at the same time friendly and obedient. Increasingly, the breed is finding favour as a companion in the home.

The tall, sophisticated Weimaraner has a short glossy coat with a silvery sheen. It is a confident and assertive dog that requires firm handling.

Chapter Six
TOY DOGS

Some groups – the hounds, the gun dogs and the terrier group, for instance – contain dogs that share common characteristics. Within each of these groups, therefore, we find dogs with either an inbuilt tendency to hunt, or to retrieve, or to go to earth in pursuit of quarry. The toy group also includes dogs that have an overriding characteristic in common – the fact that they are all small – even if they come in a variety of different shapes. In this respect, therefore, the toy group has a common link with the aforementioned groups, yet also has similarities with the working dog group and the utility dog group, both of which also have a heterogeneous collection of breeds within them.

The dogs in the toy group have also been bred with a different purpose in mind. Although many breeds within the other groups are kept solely as pets, their original purpose is to perform some kind of work. Toy dogs are bred primarily to be companions (although many of them also make excellent watchdogs and some may catch vermin very adequately).

Despite their small size, toy dogs are still dogs, and they should be treated as such. They may not need to expend as much energy as some other breeds, but they still need adequate amounts of exercise and a correct canine diet; being carried around all day and fed sweets and other inappropriate food is a demeaning

way to treat a dog. Given the chance, most toy breeds will enjoy a romp in the open air and can normally give a good account of themselves when confronted by larger varieties of their species. A properly treated dog, whatever its size, will pay back the kindness shown to it with affection and by being an amusing

Charles Spaniel and the Cavalier King Charles Spaniel, while lovers of spitz-type dogs will find the Pomeranian has all the spark and energy, together with the voice, of its larger cousins.

Exotic, long-coated dogs come no better than in the form of the Papillon, Pekingese and Havanese, while for grace and elegance it would be hard to find a better example than the Italian Greyhound – truly a Greyhound in miniature. And for sheer character and a look of pure mischief on its face, nothing can beat the Griffon Bruxellois.

OPPOSITE BELOW: Despite its diminutive size, the Chihuahua is a spirited and intelligent dog that moves in a swift and purposeful way.

LEFT: When prepared for a show, groomed impeccably and with bows in its hair, it is easy to forget that the Yorkie is a typical terrier, bred originally for work and still full of energy and ready for action.

BELOW: The Havanese is a tough little character that can stand up for itself in most situations but fits well into family life.

and stimulating companion. Most toy breeds are highly intelligent and can be quickly trained. Another feature shared by most toy dogs is that they are attractive, neat-looking animals.

The toy group has representatives drawn from many other breed types, as well as some that are unique to the group. The terriers have representatives in the shape of the Affenpinscher, the Australian Silky Terrier, the English Toy Terrier, the Yorkshire Terrier, and the Miniature Pinscher. These dogs, although they may be small, all have the typical terrier characteristics of bravery and dash.

For admirers of spaniels the choice in the toy group includes the King

AFFENPINSCHER

There is some disagreement concerning the exact origins of the Affenpinscher, with some authorities believing it to be a descendant of wire-coated terriers from Scandinavia, while others think the dog has a link with Asiatic breeds. The dog in its present form is regarded as coming out of Germany, where it has been known for centuries and where it is also known as the Black Devil because of its mischievous expression.

A rough-coated, robust-looking dog with a monkey-like face, the head has a rather broad skull and a short, blunt muzzle. The nose is black. The dark, round eyes have a certain glint to them. The ears are small and may be drop or erect. The short neck is carried

on a body with a short, straight back. The legs are straight, and the tail is carried high.

The coat is short, dense, hard and wiry; the head has prominent whiskers. The colour is usually black, but there may also be grey in the coat.

Full of character and energy, the Affenpinscher is a delightful small companion dog that will fearlessly confront any uninvited visitor arriving at the door.

Also known as the Black Devil, on account of its mischievous expression, the plucky Affenpinscher makes an excellent companion and watchdog and is quick to see off strangers.

AUSTRALIAN SILKY TERRIER

The breed came about in the 1800s as the result of crossings between Yorkshire and Australian Terriers. It was formerly known as the Sydney Silky Terrier, after a well-known breeder of these dogs moved to the city of that name with his kennels.

This is a low-slung, long-coated dog with a refined look about it. The head is wedge-shaped, with a moderate to broad, flat skull. The nose is black. The eyes are round, small and have an alert expression. The ears are V-shaped and pricked. The neck is slightly arched and is carried on a longish body. The legs are short and finely-boned. The tail is usually docked and carried erect.

The coat is fine, straight, long and glossy with a silky texture. Colours are blue-and-tan and grey-blue-and-tan.

The long, fine coat and generally elegant appearance of this breed should not disguise the fact that the Silky is a real terrier! Keen, active and ready for anything, the dog makes a friendly companion that has plenty of stamina.

The Australian Silky Terrier has all its 'terrier' instincts still intact, despite its elegant appearance, being a lively, plucky little dog with plenty of energy.

BICHON FRISÉ

This sprightly little dog came from the area of the Mediterranean, possibly as long ago as the 14th century, and later found favour at the royal courts of Europe. After the French Revolution, the dog became a familiar part of circus acts, but by the 19th century its popularity had declined. The breed's fortunes were restored, however, when it was recognized by the French Kennel Club in 1934.

A sturdy, lively little dog with a thick woolly coat. The head has a broad skull with a shortish muzzle. The nose is black. The eyes are large, dark, round, and prominently forward-facing, their expression being one of alertness. The ears are pendulous. An arched, moderate to long neck is carried on a body with a well-developed chest and broad loins. The legs are straight and well-boned. The tail is usually carried in a curve over the back.

The coat is thick, silky and loosely curled; the coat is often clipped into a distinctive shape. The colour should be solid white.

Lively and confident, the Bichon Frisé is happiest when receiving plenty of attention from its owner. It likes to join in family games and is undemanding in terms of both diet and exercise.

The enchanting little Bichon Frisé is an undemanding pet which enjoys all the bustle of family life. However, the coat requires regular grooming to retain its beautiful appearance.

BOLOGNESE

The city of Bologna in northern Italy gives its name to this dog. Similar in style to many of the bichon breeds, the Bolognese has existed in Italy for hundreds of years but is relatively rare elsewhere. The dog is also known as the Bichon Bolognese.

A compact, squarely-built dog with a distinctive coat, the head has a broad skull and a short, strong muzzle. The nose is black. The eyes are large, round and dark in colour. The ears are long and pendulous and are carried in such a way as to make the head appear wider than it actually is. The neck is of medium length. The body has a level back and slightly arched loins and is carried on short, well-muscled legs. The tail is carried curled over the back.

The coat is long, dense and curly, being somewhat shorter and softer on the muzzle. The colour should be pure white.

The Bolognese is another small breed that likes to take part in as many activities as possible. Intelligent and affectionate, the breed is unusual among toy breeds in that the coat is left untrimmed – although certainly not ungroomed – giving it the look of being slightly 'unkempt'.

The Bolognese is a compact, squarely-built dog.

CAVALIER KING CHARLES SPANIEL

This breed has been known for several centuries, and was a popular dog in European courts in the 17th century. Larger than its close relative, the King Charles Spaniel, and with less of a snub nose, the Cavalier King Charles Spaniel achieved British Kennel Club recognition in the 1940s.

An attractive, well-balanced small spaniel, the head has a flattish skull and a short, square muzzle. The nose is black. The large, round eyes are dark in colour and have a trusting, endearing look to them. The ears are long and pendulous, with good feathering. The neck is of medium length and slightly arched. The body is short with a level back and is carried on moderately-

boned legs. The tail is fairly long, although it is sometimes docked by one-third.

The dog has a long and silky coat, sometimes with a slight wave; there is ample feathering. Colours are black-and-tan, ruby (rich red), Blenheim (chestnut-and-white) or tricolour (black, white and tan).

One of the most popular of all the toy breeds, the Cavalier King Charles Spaniel seems to have everything to offer: it is friendly, happy to run in the fields or sit by its owner's side, it is built like a true sporting dog, and is easy to feed and groom.

The Cavalier King Charles is the ideal companion. Playful and with a cheerful disposition, it loves to run around, but is equally happy sitting by its owner's side.

CHIHUAHUA

Considered to be the world's smallest breed, the dog gets its name from the Mexican state of Chihuahua where, around the mid 1890s, it first became known to the Western world – although there is evidence that it may have originally come from the Orient. Soon after, the dog was introduced into the United States, where the breed standard was improved. The Chihuahua comes in two types – smooth-coated and long-coated.

A tiny, neat-looking dog with a prominent head. The head has a broad, rounded skull and a short, pointed muzzle and a distinct stop. The large, round eyes are set well apart; several colours are possible, according to coat-colour. The distinctive ears are large and flared and set at the sides of the head. The slightly-arched neck is carried on an elongated body with a level back. The legs are moderately well-boned and of medium length. The tail is carried over the back.

Chihuahuas come in two coat types: *Smooth-coated:* Smooth, soft and glossy. *Long-coated:* Soft and flat or wavy; there is feathering on the feet, legs and ruff. Any colour is permissible.

Despite its diminutive size, the Chihuahua is a spirited and intelligent dog that moves with a swift and purposeful action. It is friendly but will raise the alarm at the approach of unknown visitors. Although undemanding to feed, groom and exercise, the dog is not suitable for small children.

The Chihuahua, despite its small stature, has a brave spirit and a large heart. It requires little food or exercise and makes the ideal pet for an elderly person.

CHINESE CRESTED DOG

A favourite dog of the Han Dynasty in ancient China, the Chinese Crested was used to guard treasure and even in some forms of hunting. The dog was first shown in America in 1885. The breed comes in two coat forms: the hairless (with a crest of hair on the head, hair covering parts of the legs and feet and a plume of hair on the tail) and the powder puff (with a body covered in fine hair).

Active and graceful, the head has a moderate to broad, elongated skull and a medium to long, tapering muzzle. The nose may be any colour. The almond-shaped eyes are almost black and are set widely apart. The large ears are held erect in the hairless variety, but drop ears are permitted in the powder puff.

The neck is long and lean. The body is of medium length with a deep chest. The legs are long and lightly-boned and end in hare-like feet. The tail is long and tapering.

The dog comes in two coat-types: *Hairless:* Hair confined to head crest, lower legs and feet and tail plume; the skin may be plain or spotted and may lighten in summer. *Powder puff:* The coat consists of a soft veil of long hair. Any colour is permitted.

Happy, lively and affectionate, the Chinese Crested Dog is a tough breed that keeps itself very clean and enjoys reasonable amounts of exercise. The hairless variety needs to be protected from sunburn.

The Chinese Crested Dog is an ancient breed from the Han Dynasty, and if you are looking for an unusual pet, then this is the one for you.

ENGLISH TOY TERRIER

The English Toy Terrier, once known as the Toy Black-and-Tan Terrier, has an ancestry which includes Black-and-Tan Terriers and Italian Greyhounds. The English Toy Terrier was a familiar sight in rat pits during Regency and Georgian periods, where this active little dog would work against the clock, with wagers having been placed on the number of rats it could kill in an allotted time.

A well-balanced, elegant and compact toy dog, reminiscent of a small, prick-eared Manchester Terrier. The head has a long, flat and narrow skull and a narrowing muzzle. The nose is black. The almond-shaped eyes are small and dark with a bright and lively expression. The ears are held erect by the time the dog is mature, and are described as 'candle-flame' in shape. The long, arched neck is carried on a short body with a slightly curving back and a deep, narrow chest. The legs are long and fine-boned. The tail is long and tapering.

The coat is thick, close, smooth and glossy. Colour is black-and-tan; the

The English Toy Terrier has a beautiful flowing action when it moves. It is alert and intelligent, makes a delightful pet, and is a good rodent deterrent.

standard is very precise about the distribution of the tan markings.

A sound example of this breed moves with a smooth, flowing action and is a delight to watch. The English Toy Terrier has all the characteristics of a true terrier: alertness, speed of movement and excellent vermin-catching qualities. It is also friendly and watchful.

The Griffon Bruxellois was bred to catch rats and guard property. As its name suggests, it originated in Belgium, taking its name from the city of Brussels. It has a lively, alert and mischievous nature and makes a delightful pet.

walrus moustache. *Smooth-coated:* The coat is short and tight.

No other dog has such a mischievous face, and this is especially apparent in the rough-coated variety. Lively, fearless and alert, the Griffon Bruxellois makes a happy and amusing pet dog for both country- and town-dwellers.

GRIFFON BRUXELLOIS

Coming from Belgium, where it was used in stables for keeping down vermin and for raising the alarm if anyone approached, dogs very similar to the Griffon Bruxellois were depicted in paintings in the 1400s, and the breed was well established in the 1600s. There is a mixture of breeds in its ancestry, including Affenpinscher, Pug, and various terriers. Two varieties exist – a rough-coated form and a smooth-coated form called the Petit Brabançon.

A square, well-built little dog with a monkey-like face. The head has a broad, round skull, a short, wide muzzle, and a prominent chin. The nose is black. The eyes are large and round. The ears are semi-erect. The medium-length neck is slightly arched, and the deep-chested body is carried on straight, medium-length legs. The tail is usually docked.

The dog come in two coat types: *Rough-coated:* The coat is hard and wiry, but not curly, with a prominent

HAVANESE

The national dog of Cuba, the Havanese was probably brought to the country by traders or Spanish colonists. Many of these dogs were subsequently taken to the United States when their owners fled the Cuban Communist revolution. The dog is also known as the Bichon Havanais.

A long-coated, well-built, bichon-type dog. The head has a broad skull, a pointed muzzle, and a moderate stop. The nose is usually black, but may be brown to tone with some coat-colours. The large, almond-shaped eyes are dark and have a kindly expression. The drop ears are moderately-pointed. The neck is of medium length, and the body has a level topline with a slight rise over the loins. The legs are fairly short and medium-boned, ending in hare-like feet. The tail, usually carried high over the back, is covered in long, silky hair.

The coat is soft and silky, with a dense crest on the head. Any colour is permitted, including white, cream, black, blue, chocolate or silver.

Friendly, lively and intelligent, the Havanese is a tough little character that can stand up for itself in most situations but fits well into family life.

Also known as the Bichon Havanais, the Havanese is the national dog of Cuba. It may look cute and pretty, but it is a tough little character that knowns how to look after itself.

ITALIAN GREYHOUND

Dogs very similar in appearance to this breed can be seen depicted in the tombs of ancient pharaohs, although the modern Italian Greyhound was probably bred more recently in Roman times. This is the smallest of the sighthounds, and its diminutive size precludes serious chasing as part of a hunt. Instead, it is admired for its small-scale elegance, easy maintenance, and gentle nature.

A Greyhound in miniature, the head has a long, flat, narrow skull and a fine, long muzzle. The nose may be any dark colour. The eyes are expressive, large and bright. The delicate, rose-shaped ears are set well back on the head. The long neck is gracefully arched and is carried on a narrow, deep-chested body; the back is slightly arched over the loins. The legs are long and well-muscled and end in hare-like feet. The tail is long, fine and carried low.

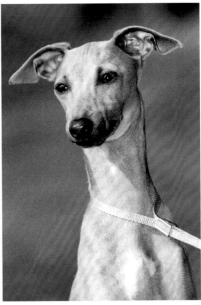

The coat is satin-like, fine and short. Colours are black, blue, cream, fawn, red, white – or any of these colours with white.

Despite its fragile appearance, the Italian Greyhound is brave and energetic. It has a good turn of speed over terrain, moving with the same long-striding gait as its larger cousin. The dog is also affectionate, being quite happy to sit at home next to its owner.

The Italian Greyhound is a perfect miniature of its larger cousin. However, it is quiet and gentle and would perhaps feel happier in a home that contains no young children.

The Japanese Chin is the perfect pet for those unable to walk too far. The coat needs regular grooming to keep it in good condition.

The coat is long, silky, soft, straight and profuse. Colours are black-and-white or red-and-white.

The Japanese Chin is a tiny dog with a cheerful and friendly nature. The breed's characteristic facial expression is one suggesting surprise. Although happy to go for leisurely walks, it is unfair to expect it to undertake anything too demanding. To keep it in good condition, the coat needs to be regularly groomed.

JAPANESE CHIN

This attractive little dog is also known as the Japanese Spaniel, although it has a strong resemblance to the Pekingese. The breed probably arrived in Japan as a gift from the Chinese royal court.

This is a lively and dainty little dog with a distinctive face. The head is large, with a broad skull, rounded in front, and with a short, wide muzzle and deep stop. The nose is usually black, but in reds and whites it may be of a colour harmonizing with the coat. The eyes are large and dark and set widely apart. The small, V-shaped ears are well-feathered. The body is compact with a broad chest, and is carried on straight, fine-boned legs ending in hare-like feet. The tail is well-feathered and carried curved over the back.

KING CHARLES SPANIEL

Also known as the English Toy Spaniel, the King Charles Spaniel is so named because it was a favourite at the court of the English King Charles II. Many paintings from the period also depict one or more of these spaniels somewhere in the scene, such was their popularity. This spaniel is closely related to the Cavalier King Charles Spaniel. The King Charles Spaniel, however, has a shorter nose and a slightly more domed skull than the Cavalier.

A cobby and aristocratic-looking small dog. The head has a broad, arched skull and a short, square, upturned muzzle. The nose is black. The eyes are large, set widely apart, and have a friendly expression. The well-feathered ears are long and pendulous. The arched neck is carried on a broad,

deep-chested body. The legs are short and straight. The tail, also well-feathered, may be docked.

The coat is long, silky and straight. Colours are black-and-tan, ruby (rich red), Blenheim (chestnut-and-white) or tricolour (black, white and tan).

The King Charles Spaniel is undemanding both in terms of feeding and exercise. It is an appealing little dog with a gentle and affectionate nature.

The King Charles Spaniel was the preferred pet of the English King Charles II, so it has been around for quite a long time. It is much in evidence in the paintings of the period.

LÖWCHEN (LITTLE LION DOG)

The Löwchen has been known in European countries such as France, Spain and Germany since the 1500s. By 1960, however, its popularity had declined to such an extent that it was listed as the rarest dog in the world – although numbers have improved since that time, and the breed has gained new fans. This bichon-type breed gets its other name, Little Lion, because of the characteristic lion-like shape into which its coat is sometimes trimmed.

A well-built, active dog with a coat clipped into a shape resembling that of a lion. The head is short and broad, with a flat skull, a short, strong muzzle, and a well-defined stop. The eyes are large and round, with an intelligent expression. The ears are pendent. The body is short and strong and is carried

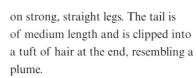

on strong, straight legs. The tail is of medium length and is clipped into a tuft of hair at the end, resembling a plume.

The coat is long and wavy. Any colours are permissible.

A friendly, lively and intelligent little dog, the Löwchen makes a good family pet and is robust enough to enjoy plenty of rough-and-tumble when there are children about.

Although it has been known in Europe for centuries, the Löwchen is rapidly gaining popularity elsewhere. Eager to please, lively and intelligent, this is a fun dog that all the family can enjoy.

MALTESE

The Maltese, or Maltese Terrier, is one of the oldest breeds in Europe, probably introduced to Malta by Phoenicians trading around the Mediterranean. There is evidence of the dog being admired by early civilizations such as the ancient Greeks, and the Romans also kept these small dogs as pets, before they eventually became popular again during the Middle Ages.

This is a neat little dog with an abundant white coat. The head has a flat skull and a short, broad muzzle. The nose is black. The eyes are dark brown and have an intelligent expression. The ears are long, well-feathered and pendulous. The body is short and cobby and carried on

short, straight legs. The tail, also well-feathered, is carried arched over the back.

The coat is long, straight and silky. The colour should be pure white, although occasional lemon markings can appear.

The Maltese moves with a free-flowing action, seeming to glide along with the coat wafting around its body. Although small, this is a tough, friendly and alert dog that likes to play and enjoys exercise. The coat needs plenty of grooming to keep it in peak condition.

The Maltese has been celebrated since Roman times, when it was especially favoured by women. It may have a feminine appearance, but it is a tough little dog for all that.

MINIATURE PINSCHER

A German breed, the Miniature Pinscher, as the name suggests, is the smallest of the pinschers, having been bred from German terriers about 100 years ago. Today, the Miniature is a widely popular dog.

A compact, elegant, smooth-coated small dog, the head is long with a flat skull and a strong muzzle. The nose is usually black, but in blue- or chocolate-coated dogs it may harmonize with the coat-colour. The eyes are usually black. The ears may be carried erect or in a half-dropped position. The neck is graceful and arched and is carried on a short, moderately deep-chested body. The legs are straight and medium-boned. The tail may be docked short or left natural (if the latter, it is often carried arched over the body).

The coat is smooth, straight, hard and glossy. Colours are black, blue, chocolate with tan markings, or various shades of red.

Small it may be, but the Miniature Pinscher is a fearless, active and alert little dog. It moves with a characteristic, high-stepping gait, and also has remarkable hearing, barking to alert the household of a stranger's approach.

Despite its small stature, the Minature Pinscher has lost none of the bravery and alertness of its larger cousins.

PAPILLON

The Papillon, also known as the Butterfly Dog because of the shape of its ears, is recognized as a Franco-Belgian breed. In fact, there are two versions of this dog – one with erect ears (the origin of the name 'Papillon') and the other with drop ears. Once popular in the royal courts of Europe, the dog is still much admired today.

An alert, silky-coated dog, the head has a slightly rounded skull and a pointed muzzle with a well-defined stop. The nose is black. The medium-sized eyes are dark and alert. The ears are of two types: either erect and held like the open wings of a butterfly, or carried dropped; in either style the ears are well-fringed with hair. The body is long, with a level back, and is carried on finely-boned legs that end in hare-like feet. The long tail is carried arched over the back and falling to one side.

The coat is full, flowing, long and silky; the chest has an abundant frill. The coat is white with patches of any

colour except liver; the preferred markings on the head include a white stripe down the centre of the skull that helps to accentuate the butterfly effect.

Intelligent, affectionate and easy to train, the attractive little Papillon is a star performer in obedience tests. The dog is a delightful companion, but is not recommended as a pet for small children.

The charming Papillon remains the heart-stealer it was when it was a favourite of European royalty. Today, it is still admired for its playfulness and strong sense of fun.

The Pekingese is not the most active of dogs and is content to amble along at its own pace. It does, however, require regular grooming to prevent the long coat from becoming hopelessly matted.

PEKINGESE

Once the sacred dog of China and named after the capital city of that country, this little dog is another of those breeds that is recognized by people the world over. Its ancestry can be traced back to at least the 8th-century Tang Dynasty, and for centuries it was highly prized at the Imperial Court. Perhaps this royal patronage explains the sense of self-importance which the Pekingese seems to convey. In the 1860s, some examples of the breed were brought to England after Peking was overrun, and in the early 1900s it was introduced to America.

A small, well-balanced and long-coated dog with a characteristic monkey face. The head is large, with a broad skull and a short, broad, wrinkled muzzle with a strong underjaw. The flat nose is black. The eyes are large and round. The ears are heart-shaped and pendulous. The short neck is carried on a short body with a broad chest. The short legs are well-boned, the hind legs being somewhat lighter. The well-feathered tail is carried curled tightly over one side of the back.

The outercoat is long and thick with a full mane and good feathering on the ears, legs, tail and feet; there is a thick undercoat. All colours are permitted except liver and albino.

Playful and fearless, the Pekingese is also an affectionate dog that makes a highly individual pet. However, this is not a breed that takes kindly to long walks in the country, preferring instead to amble along at its own pace with its characteristic rolling gait. The coat needs plenty of regular grooming to keep it in peak condition.

POMERANIAN

This is the smallest of the spitz-type dogs and is a descendant of the big sled-pulling dogs of the Arctic region. This German dog came to Britain in the late 1870s, and its popularity later received a boost when Queen Victoria decide to keep examples of the breed.

A small, compact, fox-faced dog with an abundant coat. The head has a slightly flat skull and a short, pointed muzzle. The nose is black in white, sable or orange dogs, brown in chocolate-tipped sable dogs, and self-coloured in dogs with other coat-colours. The eyes are bright and dark with an intelligent expression. The ears are small and held erect. The body is short, with a deep chest, and is carried on fine-boned, medium-length legs. The tail is carried over the back in typical spitz fashion.

The outercoat is long, straight and harsh, being very thick around the neck

and shoulders; the undercoat is soft and thick. All colours are permitted, including white, black, cream, brown, orange, beaver and sable.

Pomeranians have plenty of energy, like their larger cousins. Extroverted and vivacious, the dog makes a lively companion. It also has a shrill bark to alert its owner when anyone approaches the house.

Like all spitz-type dogs, the Pomeranian – the smallest of the breed – has a good deal of energy and vivacity. It makes a lively little companion and its high-pitched bark acts as a good burglar alarm.

PUG

The Pug is thought to have originated in China, where the dog was the companion of monks. It arrived in Europe with traders in the 1500s and subsequently became very popular in the Netherlands and in Britain.

This is a square, muscular dog reminiscent of a miniature mastiff. The head is large and round with a short, blunt muzzle; the skin has clearly-defined wrinkles. The huge, dark eyes are set in the sockets in a way that makes them seem globular; they are also highly expressive. The ears are small and thin, and there are two types: drop rose ears or folded button ears, the latter being preferred. The neck is strong and thick and is carried on a short, wide-chested body. The fairly long legs are strong and straight. The tail is curled tightly over the hip.

The Pug has a coat which is short, smooth, soft and glossy. Colours are silver, fawn, apricot, or black; light colours should have clearly contrasting markings, including a dark mask and ears.

The sturdy Pug is a real character among dogs. The body language and the almost talking eyes can express all manner of moods, from alert watchfulness to an appealing request for attention. A playful and hardy dog, the Pug enjoys exercise and is easy to feed and groom.

The Pug is a sturdy, muscular little dog, rather like a miniature mastiff. It may look tough but it is actually quite a softie, being gentle, even-tempered and patient with children.

YORKSHIRE TERRIER

The result of crossings involving the Black-and-Tan Terrier, the Skye Terrier, the Dandie Dinmont and the Maltese, the 'Yorkie' first came to prominence in the 1850s. The Yorkshire Terrier was originally bred as a rat-fighting dog, at which time the breed was larger than the show and pet dogs seen today.

A compact, long-coated small terrier, the head is quite small with a flattish skull and a short muzzle. The nose is black. The dark eyes are medium-sized and have an intelligent, alert expression. The small V-shaped ears are carried erect. The compact body has a level back and is carried on shortish, straight legs. The tail is usually docked to measure about half its natural length.

The coat is long, straight and glossy with a silky texture; the hair is longer on the head. The main body colour is dark steel-blue, the hair on the head being a rich golden-tan, and the hair on the chest a bright tan.

Despite its dainty and feminine appearance, the Yorkshire Terrier is a true terrier at heart, having been bred to fight rats. It is alert and spirited and ready for action at any time.

Groomed to the peak of perfection for the show ring, it is hard to believe that this dog, with its lustrous, flowing coat and colourful bows in its hair, is also a typical terrier. This means that it is tough, brave, and ready to spring into action whenever the opportunity presents itself.

INDEX

DOGS

INDEX & ACKNOWLEDGEMENTS

All pictures in this book are supplied
courtesy of the RSPCA Picture
Library, with the exception of the
following, which are supplied by Cogis:
pages 105 left, 110, 111 right, 112 left,
113, 115 left, 117 right, 119 right, 123
left, 124, 136 right, 145 both, 151 left,
157 both, 160 both, 163 left, 183 right,
184, 214 right, 235, 244 both.